PLAYS FROM

Fairy Tales

Grades K – 3

DEDICATION

This book is dedicated to my parents, grandparents, aunts and uncles from whom I first heard fairy tales as a child...and to my wife, Jane, who makes every day a fairy tale come true.

Published by Smith and Kraus, Inc.
PO Box 127, Lyme, NH 03768
Copyright ©1997 by L.E. McCullough

Manufactured in the United States of America
First Edition: May 1997
10 9 8 7 6 5 4 3 2
Cover and Text Design by Julia Hill/Freedom Hill Design
Cover Illustration by Aline Ordman

The Library of Congress Cataloging-In-Publication Data
McCullough, L.E.
        Plays from fairy tales: grades K–3 / L.E. McCullough. —1st ed.
        p. cm. — (Young actors series)
Includes bibliographical references.
Summary: Presents twelve original plays that are adaptions of fairy tales from around the world.
ISBN 1-57525-109-4
1. Children's plays, American. 2. Fairy tales—Adaptions. [1. Fairy tales—drama. 2. Folklore—Drama. 3. Plays.] I. Title. II. Series.
PS3563.C35297P54   1997
812'.54—dc21   97-32881
                                CIP
                                AC

PLAYS FROM
Fairy Tales

Grades K – 3

L.E. McCullough

YOUNG ACTORS SERIES

SK
A Smith and Kraus Book

A NOTE ON COSTUMES, SETS, AND MUSIC

Most fairy tales are set in a "legendary time" that most closely corresponds in real cultural and costume details to the early Middle Ages, c. 800-1200 A.D. For stories set in specific countries, books on ethnic dress can be consulted as well. Dover Books publishes several good collections of period costumes, two of which are:

• *What People Wore: A Visual History of Dress from Ancient Times to 20th-Century America.* Douglas Gorsline. This has a huge bibliography of other costume books.
• *Historic Costume in Pictures.* Braun & Schneider. New York, NY: Dover Books.

To decorate your scrims and background sets, Dover also publishes iron-on transfer books of gargoyles and medieval folklore creatures, angels, wild animals — plus calligraphy, floral patterns and ornamental designs from cultures around the world including African, Asian, Celtic, American Indian, Old European and more.

If you'd like some costuming ideas for fairies, ogres, trolls, witches and so on, check out these books:

• *Abbey Lubbers, Banshees & Boggarts: An Illustrated Encyclopedia of Fairies.* Katharine Mary Briggs, illustrated by Yvonne Gilbert. New York, NY: Pantheon Books.
• *Mythical and Fabulous Creatures: A Source Book and Research Guide.* Malcolm South, editor. New York, NY: P. Bedrick Books.
• *Faeries, Described and Illustrated.* Brian Froud and Alan Lee. New York, NY: Abrams.
• *Fians, Fairies, and Picts.* David MacRitchie. Norwood, PA: Norwood Editions.
• *The World Guide to Gnomes, Fairies, Elves, and Other Little People.* Thomas Keightley. New York, NY: Avenel Books.
• *Fairies and Elves.* Chicago, IL: Time-Life Books.
• *Gnomes.* Wil Huygen, illustrated by Rien Poortvliet. New York, NY: Peacock Press.

Using authentic ethnic or period music is a great way to enhance your production. The public library is always a good source, yet recordings of folk and ethnic international music are increasingly more available at mainstream record stores and from catalogues. If you have questions about where to find recordings or written music of the tunes or genres included in these plays, or want some tips on performing and arranging them, I would be happy to assist you and may be reached by e-mail at: FEADANISTE@AOL.COM.

CONTENTS

FOREWORD

My first and last philosophy, that which I believe in with
unbroken certainty, I learnt in the nursery...The things I
believed most in then, the things I believe in now, are the
things called fairy tales.

> — *G. K. Chesterton (1874–1936)*
> *English essayist and novelist*

The twelve plays in this book celebrate one of the most happy
occurrences of childhood the world over — the telling and hearing of fairy tales. As many modern writers have shown, fairy tales
are not simply escapist fantasy; they are one of the chief ways a child
learns about the adult world and how to live in it.

In his landmark volume *The Uses of Enchantment: The Meaning and
Importance of Fairy Tales,* psychologist Bruno Bettelheim explored the
deep, subconscious terrain of the fairy tale. "Fairy tales direct the child to
discover his identity and calling, and they also suggest what experiences
are needed to develop his character further."[1] Fairy tales hold out the
belief that, despite adversity, a good, happy life is within our grasp — but
only if we face and surmount struggles in the outside world and within our
own selves. Benevolent powers (fairy godmothers, talking animals, singing
swords, magic beans, etc.) will aid us in this search, but we must be bold
and resolute; the timid and narrow-minded inevitably fail. With their ele-
gant, magical simplicity, fairy tales illustrate a child's inner conflicts while
pointing out how these conflicts might be resolved in symbolic terms that
correspond to the juvenile worldview.

No one knows who or what people told the first fairy tales, though the
elements of the Cinderella story have been found in an Egyptian legend
(*Rhodopis and Her Gilded Sandals*) dating from the thirteenth century
before Christ; other well-known tales are rooted in the mythology of
ancient Greek and Indian mythology. With remarkable resilience and

adaptability, stock fairy tale characters and situations have traversed not just the barriers of time but of space and language — the *Little Red Riding Hood* story is found in Africa as well as northern Europe...the *Frog Prince* cycle turns up across Eurasia from India to England...variants of *Hansel and Gretel* are known in Europe, Japan, India, Africa, the Pacific Islands and among North American Indians.

Plays from Fairy Tales have been designed to combine with studies in other disciplines: history, science, language, dance, music, social studies, etc. *A Cosmic Bouquet* can supplement lesson plans in astronomy and science. *The Twelve Months* can generate a pre- or post-play discussion about the evolution of time and calendar measurement. Most of the plays are originally from non-English-speaking peoples; feel free to have the characters speak a few additional lines of the native language, and decorate the set with architecture, plants and art objects specific to that region. If you are a music teacher and want to add songs and music to any of the plays, go ahead and make it a class project by organizing a chorus or having students select appropriate recordings from the host culture to play before and after the performance.

Besides those children enrolled in the onstage cast, others can be included in the production as lighting and sound technicians, prop masters, script coaches and stage managers. *Plays from Fairy Tales* is an excellent vehicle for getting other members of the school and community involved in your project. Maybe there are ethnic dance troupes or accomplished performers of ethnic music in your area; ask them to give a special concert or lecture when you present the play. There are undoubtedly several knowledgeable scholars at your local historical society, library, art museum, high school and college who can add interesting tidbits about the customs and folklore that provide background for these tales. Try utilizing the talents of local school or youth orchestra members to play incidental music...get the school art club to paint scrims and backdrops...see if a senior citizens' group might volunteer time to sew costumes...inquire whether any local restaurants might bring samples of ethnic cuisine.

Most of all, have lots of fun. Realizing that many performing groups may have limited technical and space resources, I have kept sets, costumes and props minimal. However, if you do have the ability to build an entire wooden sailing ship for *The Great Flying Ship of Ivan the Impossible* or fashion a facsimile of an underground palace for *The Lost Spear* — go for it! Adding more music and dance and visual arts and crafts into the production involves more children and makes your play a genuinely multi-media event.

Similarly, I have supplied only basic stage and lighting directions. Blocking is really the province of the director; once you get the play up and moving, feel free to suit cast and action to your available population and experience level of actors. When figuring out how to stage these plays, I suggest you follow the venerable UYI Method — Use Your Imagination. If the play calls for a boat, bring in a wood frame, an old bathtub or have children draw a boat and hang as a scrim behind where the actors perform. Keep in mind the spirit of the old Andy Hardy musicals: "C'mon, everybody! Let's make a show!"

Age and gender. Obviously, your purpose in putting on the play is to entertain as well as educate; even though one typically thinks of castle guards and king's soldiers as being male, there is no reason these roles can't be played in your production by females; likewise for witches, ogres and trolls. After all, the essence of the theatrical experience is to suspend us in time and ask us to believe that anything may be possible. Once again, UYI! Adult characters, such as grandparents and "old wise men/women" can certainly be played by children costumed or made up to fit the part as closely as possible, or they can actually be played by adults. While *Plays from Fairy Tales* are intended to be performed chiefly by children, moderate adult involvement will add validation and let children know this isn't just a "kid project." If you want to get very highly choreographed or musically intensive, you will probably find a strategically placed onstage adult or two very helpful in keeping things moving smoothly. Still, never underestimate the capacity for even the youngest children to amaze you with their skill and ingenuity in making a show blossom.

Plays from Fairy Tales is a great way to enhance one of the richest literary and learning experiences in which a child can participate. And for adults, these plays offer a chance to recapture the joy and excitement we all felt the first time we heard the thrilling words "once upon a time..." Who says you can't be a kid again? Just step on board this magic carpet and follow the big blue genie...mind that dragon lurking round the corner!

L.E. McCullough, Ph.D.
Humanities Theatre Group
Indiana University-Purdue
University at Indianapolis
Indianapolis, Indiana

[1.] Bruno Bettelheim. *The Uses of Enchantment: The Meaning and Importance of Fairy Tales.* New York: Alfred A. Knopf, 1975, page 24.

Aruman, Hero of Java

In this hero tale from Java, young Aruman must prove himself worthy to succeed his father as chief — a common test in fairy tales the world over. As part of the vast Pacific island nation of Indonesia, Java has long been a meeting place and melting pot of many cultures including those of India, China, Arabia, Phillipines, Japan and, since the 1500s, Western Europe. In Javanese folklore, animals play a major role. Birds (the Black Bird in this story) are thought to be the assistants of gods; tigers are spirit carriers who guide the living to the after world. The flying shoes and cloak Aruman obtains are reminiscent of stories about other heroes such as Hermes, Perseus and the seven-league boots of the Norse messenger god Hermod.

RUNNING TIME: 15 minutes

PLACE: Java

CAST: 16 actors, min. 3 boys, 3 girls

Sumarr, the Nurse	Drahman, Aruman's Father
Aruman	Alligator
Captain	2 Sailors
Old Woman	4 Headless Dwarves
Black Bird	Maiden/Princess
2 Tigers	

STAGE SET: log or stool at down right

PROPS: tinwhistle, gold slippers, silver cloak, kriss (long curved dagger), pebbles

COSTUMES: Aruman, Sumarr, Drahman, Old Woman, Maiden wear one-piece robes or smocks and sandals; Drahman might have an accessory that indicates rank as chieftain, such as a headdress or feathered necklace; Captain and Sailors dress as pirates with boots, sashes, head kerchiefs; Headless Dwarves wear ragged clothing and a headpiece that suggests they are headless; Alligator, Black Bird, Tigers have appropriate animal masks and body coverings

(LIGHTS UP FULL. SUMARR sits at down right. Offstage left CROWD NOISE is heard.)

CROWD: *(o.s.)* Aruman! Aruman! Aruman!

SUMARR: *(to audience)* Oh, hear the people shout! They shout for Aruman, Hero of Java!

CROWD: *(o.s.)* Aruman! Aruman! Aruman!

SUMARR: Yes, many shout for Aruman, Hero of Java. I know him well. My name is Sumarr, and after his mother died, I became his nurse. And I can tell you that there was a time when no one thought this boy would grow to be a hero. Certainly not his father, Drahman, the local chief.

(DRAHMAN enters from left and strides to down center.)

DRAHMAN: *(to audience)* I am Drahman, a great chief on this island. And I fully expected my only son, Aruman, to follow in my footsteps. Yet, I fear he is weak. I fear he will not grow up to be a strong leader.

(ARUMAN enters from right, holding a tinwhistle.)

ARUMAN: Father, look at this new flute I have made from the waringin tree! *(plays a few notes)* Does it not sound beautiful?

DRAHMAN: *(turns his back to Aruman)* My son, who I wished to be a warrior, makes toys that whistle! You have disgraced me! *(exits left)*

(Aruman starts to follow Drahman but stops at down center.)

ARUMAN: Father, wait! Father, please do not be angry with me! Please, father! *(to audience)* It is no use. My father, who I wish to honor and please, believes I am a disgrace. Well, there is but one thing left to do. I will jump in the river and drown!

(Aruman runs offstage left.)

SUMARR: And that is exactly what poor Aruman did! He threw himself in the river. But instead of sinking to the bottom, he was picked up by a current that carried him downstream for many miles. When he was almost to the ocean, he was seen by a large alligator lurking along the bank.

(Aruman enters from left, rolling and sliding along his back to down center; ALLIGATOR enters from right, crawling on all fours to down center, where he regards Aruman with curiosity.)

ALLIGATOR: Hmmm. What do you know? A human boy floating down the river to the ocean. This certainly livens up my day!

ARUMAN: *(kneels and bows head)* Greetings, most honorable Alligator. Go ahead and devour me. I am so miserable, I no longer care to live one day longer.

ALLIGATOR: All in due time, all in due time. Tell me, what is that object you have at your side? A sharp-bladed kriss for tearing your enemies asunder and fighting the fierce creatures of the forest?

ARUMAN: No, honorable sir. It is a flute. *(plays a few notes)* It makes music. And music makes those who hear it joyful.

ALLIGATOR: Indeed! It makes me hungry! But if you know how to produce such joy from a stick, you cannot truly be as miserable as you say. I think you are a wizard and have come to beguile me. Therefore, I shall not eat you. Instead, I will give you these magic slippers.

(Alligator hands a pair of gold slippers to Aruman, who puts them on and stands up.)

ALLIGATOR: With these slippers you can walk on water as easily as on dry land. Try them.

ARUMAN: Thank you, I will.

(Aruman takes a large step left, then a large step right.)

ARUMAN: It is true! I *can* walk on water!

ALLIGATOR: Of course! Now walk to the ocean and seek your fortune!

(Alligator crawls off left; Aruman glides around stage.)

SUMARR: Aruman quickly reached the ocean, and he ventured out onto the boundless blue tide, just as the Alligator had told him. Aruman walked across the white waves and among all manner of fish and sea creatures for many hundreds of miles, until at last he saw a ship, whose Captain had likewise seen him.

(CAPTAIN and TWO SAILORS enter from left and spy Aruman at mid right.)

CAPTAIN: (points at Aruman) I cannot believe my eyes! Sailors, is that a boy walking across the ocean?

SAILOR #1: It looks like a boy.

SAILOR #2: But it could be a fish that resembles a boy.

CAPTAIN: Man or beast, invite him aboard!

SAILORS: Ahoy there! Ahoy!

(Aruman meets the Captain and Two Sailors at down center.)

CAPTAIN: Join us for supper and tell us of your adventures.

ARUMAN: Thank you, honorable Captain sir. I have been walking a long time.

CAPTAIN: Walking on the ocean? But how?

ARUMAN: With these magic slippers I was given from an Alligator.

SAILOR #1: Magic slippers?

SAILOR #2: From an Alligator!

SAILOR #1: The boy is mad!

SAILOR #2: Bewitched!

CAPTAIN: You know, boy, I am not sure those slippers are good for you.

ARUMAN: Not good? What do you mean?

CAPTAIN: Well, you are still a boy, and those slippers are best worn by a grown man. Some day when you feel the safest walking on water, your slippers will fail, and you will sink.

ARUMAN: What should I do?

CAPTAIN: Give me the magic slippers. In return, I will give you a magic cloak that allows you to fly in the air.

ARUMAN: Very well, that sounds like a good trade.

CAPTAIN: Sailors, fetch my cloak!

(Sailors dash off left and return with a silver cloak they put on Aruman, while Captain puts on magic slippers.)

SUMARR: In truth, the Captain had never been able to fly with the magic cloak, because he did not truly believe in its power. And so he was amazed when Aruman put on the cloak and immediately soared into the air!

(Aruman runs around stage.)

SAILOR #1: Why, the boy sails through the sky like a bird!
SAILOR #2: The cloak really is magical!
SUMARR: But when the Captain tried to walk on water with the slippers Aruman had given him, he became afraid. And his fear robbed the magic from the slippers. In an instant, he fell into the water with a loud splash!

(Captain takes tentative steps, wobbling and weaving, finally falling to floor and flailing as if swimming.)

CAPTAIN: Help! Help, I'm drowning!

(Sailors drag him to down center, where he stands and points at Aruman.)

CAPTAIN: That boy is a thief! These are not magic slippers, and he has robbed me of my magic cloak! *(draws kriss)* Sailors, capture him, and we will feed him to the sharks!

(Sailors chase Aruman but cannot catch him; they fall to their knees, exhausted, and Aruman dashes offstage right.)

CAPTAIN: You fools, he is flying away!

(Captain exits with Sailors left; Aruman enters from right, flying around stage till he stops at down center and stares at floor; OLD WOMAN and BLACK BIRD enter from left and stand at down left.)

SUMARR: And Aruman did fly away, back to Java. He flew over hills and rivers, valleys and forests. At last he flew over a very strange, very gloomy part of the land he had never seen. Even the trees drooped low to the ground and seemed on the verge of weeping. He saw a dark cave and landed near to its mouth.

ARUMAN: *(kneels, looks closer at floor)* This is a very curious cave. It is filled with darkness, as if it were the opening to an endless kingdom of night.

OLD WOMAN: Aruman!

ARUMAN: Who calls me?

OLD WOMAN: Only an old woman and her black bird!

BLACK BIRD: Squawk! Squawk!

ARUMAN: Where am I? What desolate cave is this?

OLD WOMAN: It is the deepest layer of your own heart, Aruman. It is filled with a lifetime of fears and dreams.

(Black Bird flaps wings and flies to mid center, as Aruman stares.)

BLACK BIRD: Squawk! Squawk!

ARUMAN: The bird is changing...changing into a man...a man whose face is filled with terrible sorrow and regret! *(to Old Woman)* What is the purpose of this sorcery, Old Woman?

(Old Woman throws pebbles on the ground; FOUR HEADLESS DWARVES dance out from left and cavort and shriek around Aruman.)

DWARVES: Yeeee! Yowww! Reeee! Rayyy!

ARUMAN: The Old Woman throws pebbles, and an army of headless dwarves springs to life! Begone, you phantoms!

(Aruman plays his flute at Dwarves, and they shriek and scatter offstage right; a MAIDEN enters from left and stands just at the curtain, looking at audience.)

ARUMAN: And now a lovely maiden! *(plays a few notes on flute)* Yet, she hears and sees me not.

(Maiden exits left.)

ARUMAN: Old Woman, are you a witch? Are you a spirit of the restless dead who lie buried in this ancient cave? Has my father, Drahman, sent you to torment me?

OLD WOMAN: I *am* a messenger, Aruman. And I have shown you what is the present, and what may be the future. You must now complete your journey home. For companions, I give you a pair of Tigers. By the light of their eyes, you will pass safely through the dark jungle.

(TWO TIGERS enter from left and stand on either side of Aruman.)

ARUMAN: *(bows)* I thank you, honorable messenger.

OLD WOMAN: Go, and fulfill your destiny! *(exits left)*

(Aruman and the Tigers walk slowly around the stage to stand at mid right; Drahman enters from left and stands at down center, peering out into audience.)

SUMARR: Slowly, Aruman and the Tigers made their way through the gloomy jungle. He fell many times, stumbling over rocks and vines, but the Old Woman — who was not a witch but a good fairy — watched over and protected him from harm. Finally, he arrived at the river where he had tried to kill himself. And there, standing on the bank, was his father!

ARUMAN: Father!

(Drahman turns and sees Aruman.)

ARUMAN: I see upon his face the same terrible sorrow and regret I saw on the Black Bird!

DRAHMAN: My son! You have returned!

(Aruman and Drahman embrace.)

ARUMAN: I am sorry for having disgraced you, father!

DRAHMAN: My son, it is I who have behaved in disgrace. News of your daring exploits have already reached the King of Java. He sends his daughter, the Princess, to meet you.

(The Maiden enters from left and crosses to Aruman; they bow to each other.)

ARUMAN: Why, this is the same maiden I saw in the jungle! And she is even lovelier than before!

MAIDEN: My father, the King, wishes you to come and live at our palace. Will it be your pleasure to do so?

ARUMAN: Father?

DRAHMAN: Go, my son. It is your destiny to be a hero for all Java.

(Aruman and the Maiden exit left, followed by Drahman.)

SUMARR: And so Aruman went to live in the palace, where he had many great adventures defending the kingdom. Later, he became King himself — and married the Princess.

CROWD: *(o.s.)* Aruman! Aruman! Aruman!

SUMARR: Oh, hear the people shout! They shout for Aruman, Hero of Java! The boy who was afraid of nothing — not even the deepest layers of his own heart.

CROWD: *(o.s.)* Aruman! Aruman! Aruman!

(LIGHTS OUT.)

THE END

A Cosmic Bouquet: Sun, Moon and Stars

Each day scientists learn more about the origin and nature of our physical universe — answers to the question of "how" things came to be. Fairy tales often probe deeper, by attempting to answer the question of "why" things came to be. These ancient tales from Hawaii (*The Fisherman Who Caught the Sun*), Japan (*The Moon Maiden*) and the Wasco Indians of Oregon (*Coyote Places the Stars*) offer theories about the origin of the very sun, moon and stars we see from our own earthly vantage point.

RUNNING TIME: 15 minutes

PLACE: The Cosmos Around Us

CAST: 24 actors, min. 3 boys, 3 girls

Narrator	2 Suns
3 People	Fisherman
Bamboo Cutter	Bamboo Cutter's Wife
Princess Moonbeam	Mikado
3 Soldiers	Lady of the Moon
Coyote	2 Bears
6 Wolves	

STAGE SET: a large boulder at up right

PROPS: a fisherman's net, 3 spears, bow

EFFECTS: Visual — twinkling lights that suggest fireflies at night; Sound — the *twang* or *boing* of an arrow being shot

MUSIC: *Twinkle, Twinkle, Little Star*

COSTUMES: Narrator dresses as contemporary youth; Fisherman and Three People wear one-piece robes or smocks and sandals with touches of native Hawaiian garb such as leis and shell necklaces; Two Suns can wear a blazing sun headdress and face paint with red/orange/yellow coloring; Bamboo Cutter and Bamboo Cutter's Wife dress in simple Japanese peasant clothes or one-piece robes or smocks with sandals; Mikado and Soldiers dress as Japanese samurai; Princess Moonbeam can wear a simple robe but have a sparkly headdress or glittered embroidery of some sort; Coyote, Bears and Wolves have appropriate animal masks and body coverings

---

(LIGHTS UP RIGHT. At down right NARRATOR stands and gazes skyward, humming. MUSIC: "Twinkle, Twinkle, Little Star.")

NARRATOR: *(singsong)* Twinkle, twinkle, little star; how I wonder what you are! *(to audience)* Oh, hi! I was just star gazing. And thinking about what our ancestors might have seen... others kids like us, who looked up into the sky and wondered whether the moon was made of green cheese, or whether if they really could make a wish upon a star. Well, I don't claim to have all the answers, but I've heard some good stories. Like this one from Hawaii called "The Fisherman Who Caught the Sun."

(LIGHTS FADE UP LEFT AND CENTER. At mid left are THREE PEOPLE, one standing, one kneeling, one sit-

ting, each motionless as if frozen in mid-motion of doing primitive work — hoeing or stringing beads or shelling husks. The FISHERMAN sits at mid center, a large net in his lap. SUN #1 enters from left, bows to audience, then races across stage and jumps behind boulder at up right; LIGHTS FADE TO HALF.)

NARRATOR: Many, many years ago,when People first came into the world, the Sun would burst forth from the ocean each morning and race across the sky like a bright, fiery arrow!

PERSON #1: Look! The Sun is cheating us! He flings himself across the sky and back again into the ocean before we have time to do our day's work!

PERSON #2: The Sun is not in the sky more than a couple of hours. Our crops cannot grow!

PERSON #3: We have no time to gather our food from the forest!

FISHERMAN: *(stands)* I think I shall go to the Sun and teach him to make his daily trip across the sky at the proper speed.

PERSON #1: What? You — a fisherman — are going to control the Sun?

PERSON #2: You must be mad! The salt water has gone to your brain!

PERSON #3: You will be burned to a crisp!

FISHERMAN: I do not fear the Sun. I shall catch him in this snare!

(Fisherman mimes paddling as he goes to down left, just behind stage left entrance; he sits and lies in readiness; LIGHTS FADE TO QUARTER.)

PERSON #1: The Fisherman got in his canoe and sailed out into the ocean, following the trail of the setting Sun.

PERSON #2: He sailed through the dark shadows along the silvery path of moonlight.

PERSON #3: Farther and farther he sailed to the very edge of the Earth!

PERSON #1: Until he came to the place where the Sun would burst forth the next morning and rise from the ocean.

PERSON #2: So the Fisherman waited through the long night, his snare gripped tightly in his sturdy hands.

PERSON #3: As the world slept and dreamed of Sun...

(After five seconds, LIGHTS FADE SLOWLY UP TO FULL.)

PERSON #1: At last the blackness of night dissolved into gray...

PERSON #2: Bright gems of light flashed from the ocean...

PERSON #3: Wisps of purple and rose drifted along the horizon...

PERSON #1: And a small sliver of Sun peeped up to touch the white waves...

PERSON #2: Setting the ocean aflame with blazing gold...

PERSON #3: As the Sun himself stood up and cast his light across the Earth!

(LIGHTS UP FULL as SUN #2 enters from left, bows to audience and turns to cross toward up right. Before he can start off, Fisherman throws the net over him and Sun #2 falls to knees and struggles with net as Fisherman pulls tight.)

PERSON #1: The Fisherman rose in his canoe and threw his snare over the Sun!

PERSON #2: The Sun was captured in the net!

PERSON #3: Oh, how he flamed and flared, but the Fisherman held fast!

SUN #2: Let me go, Fisherman! Or I will scorch you to bits!

FISHERMAN: Sun, from this day forth, you shall make your

way through the heavens at a proper speed! You shall give the People a fair day that is long enough to hunt and fish, build canoes and grow and gather crops!

(Sun #2 turns to Fisherman and glares, stamps feet, raises arms in gestures of anger; Sun #2 turns away from Fisherman and moves slowly toward up right, straining mightily against the net which the Fisherman uses as a farmer uses the reins of a plow.)

PERSON #1: Oh, how the Sun struggled to break free!
PERSON #2: But the Fisherman held to the ropes of the net with a grip that did not yield!
PERSON #3: And he held the Sun to a proper pace! How the People rejoiced!

(Persons #1, 2 & 3 cheer as Sun #2 stops in front of boulder, panting with exhaustion.)

SUN #2: Fisherman, I have been in the sky many hours! Let me finish my journey, so that night may fall and I may rest!
FISHERMAN: Do you promise you will no longer race wildly across the sky?
SUN #2: I promise!

(Sun #2 throws off net and exits behind boulder.)

PERSON #1: Then the Fisherman set the Sun free...
PERSON #2: But he did not take away all of the ropes.

(Fisherman places net around boulder as if securing it; LIGHTS BEGIN TO FADE OUT.)

PERSON #3: Some he left fastened to the edge of the world to remind the Sun to keep his promise.

PERSON #1: And to this very day, when the Sun rises and sets, you can still see the ropes hanging down.

PERSON #2: Some say they are the thirsty fingers of the Sun drawing water from the ocean. Look now as he sinks into the sea!

PERSON #3: But I tell you, those rays which seem to anchor the Sun to the sea are the ropes of the snare by which the brave Fisherman binds him to this very day!

(LIGHTS OUT BRIEFLY; all characters except Narrator exit. LIGHTS UP FULL. BAMBOO CUTTER and BAMBOO CUTTER'S WIFE stand at down left, miming motions of cutting and stacking bamboo; Narrator stands at down right and addresses audience.)

NARRATOR: Once upon a time in Japan, a Bamboo Cutter and his Wife lived in a great forest near the great mountain of Fujiyama. They were honest, hardworking people who loved each other very much. But their happiness was not complete, because they had no children of their own.

WIFE: Dear husband, more welcome to me than cherry blossoms in spring would be a small child of our own.

BAMBOO CUTTER: I know, my wife. But such joy is not meant for us in this lifetime. *(goes back to cutting bamboo)*

WIFE: *(kneels, looks toward boulder)* Mighty Fujiyama, I pray to you! Send a child to comfort us in our old age!

(LIGHTS FLICKER.)

WIFE: *(points to boulder)* Husband, look! On the peak of the mountain a child is beaming at us!

BAMBOO CUTTER: *(peers intently)* That is just your imagination, dear wife! I see no beam! But, I will climb the mountain and see what is up there.

(Bamboo Cutter crosses slowly to boulder, miming mountain-climbing motions.)

NARRATOR: So he followed the trail of silver light that shone through the forest, up the steep slopes of the mountain. Finally, he followed the beaming light to a tall bamboo by the bank of a mountain stream. There, in the branches of the tree, he found a tiny baby girl, more beautiful than anything he had ever seen.

(Bamboo Cutter looks behind boulder and reels back in surprise as PRINCESS MOONBEAM comes out from behind and bows.)

BAMBOO CUTTER: Who are you, shining creature?
PRINCESS MOONBEAM: I am Princess Moonbeam. The Moon is my mother, but she has sent me to Earth to comfort the lonely hearts of you and your wife.
(Bamboo Cutter takes Princess Moonbeam by the hand and walks with her to down center, where they are met by the Wife.)

BAMBOO CUTTER: Wife, Wife! See what the Moon has sent us!
WIFE: A child of our own! I am overjoyed!

(Bamboo Cutter, Wife and Princess Moonbeam sit on floor in semi-circle and mime drinking tea.)

NARRATOR: The years went by, and Princess Moonbeam grew to be a lovely women. She brought great happiness to the Bamboo Cutter and his Wife. But one day, there came riding by their cottage the mighty Mikado! The Emperor of Japan himself!

(MIKADO enters from left, followed by THREE SOLDIERS with spears; Mikado sees Princess Moonbeam.)

MIKADO: There is the most radiant creature on all the Earth! She has won my heart! I must have her for my Empress!

PRINCESS MOONBEAM: *(rises, bows to Mikado)* I am sorry, honorable sir. I, too, love you very much. But my mother the Moon is calling me, and I must return.

MIKADO: No! Stay here, beautiful Moonbeam! Stay with me here on Earth! I will place three thousand soldiers on guard to make sure no one takes you!

(Three Soldiers turn toward up right and brandish spears as Princess Moonbeam begins to whirl; LADY OF THE MOON enters from behind boulder and passes easily past Soldiers.)

NARRATOR: But when the moon rose full, a bridge of white light came down to the Earth. And the Lady of the Moon floated down, passing easily through the Soldiers to the Princess. She wrapped her Moon child in a cloak of silver mist, then led her gently back to their faraway home in the night sky.

(Lady of the Moon and Princess Moonbeam exit behind boulder, Moonbeam turning and waving sadly before exiting. LIGHTS FADE OUT SLOWLY as other characters except Narrator exit left.)

NARRATOR: As she departed, the Princess wept bright silvery tears for those she was leaving behind. And her tears took wing and floated to Earth as fireflies, carrying a message of love to comfort the Mikado and her Earthly parents.

(VISUAL EFFECT: twinkling lights on boulder.)

NARRATOR: To this very day, the gleaming tears of Princess

Moonbeam float hither and yon through the marshes and forests of Japan. And when children see a firefly, they call out:

BAMBOO CUTTER & WIFE: Princess Moonbeam! Princess Moonbeam! Please, stay and marry me!

(LIGHTS UP FULL. Narrator at down right addresses audience.)

NARRATOR: Some people believe our universe was created according to a definite plan. Maybe most of it was. But whenever the trickster Coyote got involved, accidents always tended to happen.

(SIX WOLVES enter from left and sit at down center in a semi-circle; they stare up at the sky.)

NARRATOR: A long time ago, in the land of the Wasco Indians, there were six wolves, all of them brothers. One night, while they sat looking up at the sky, Coyote came along.

(COYOTE, carrying a bow, enters from left and approaches Wolves.)

COYOTE: *(to audience)* These Wolf Brothers make me laugh! Always sitting around with their heads in the clouds or howling at the moon! Say, Wolves! What are you looking at?

WOLF #1: It's Coyote!

(Wolves look down at ground.)

WOLVES #2-6: *(mumble)* Hey, hi, oh, nothing, nope, nothing, nuh-uh…

COYOTE: Nothing? The six of you are looking up at nothing?

WOLF #2: You got it!
WOLF #3: A whole sky full of nothing!
WOLF #4: Nothing up there at all for you to see, Coyote!
WOLF #5: No, don't bother, we've already looked.
WOLF #6: See you round the mountain, Coyote!
COYOTE: Yeh, sure. See you!

(Coyote walks a few steps toward right; Wolves stare up at sky.)

COYOTE: The next night, I come along, and once again the Wolf boys are glued to the stratosphere. Say, Wolves! What are you looking at?
WOLF #1: It's Coyote again.

(Wolves look down at ground.)

WOLVES #2-6: Hey, hi, oh, nothing, nope, nothing, nuh-uh...
COYOTE: Okay, fellas. Whatever you say. *(to audience, twirling his finger against his head in the "crazy" gesture)* Mondo wacko!

(Coyote walks a few steps toward right; Wolves stare up at sky.)

COYOTE: The third night, I come along again, and would you believe it? These silly cousins of mine hadn't moved an inch! Maybe I'll play a little trick. *(points to sky)* Say, lookout! It just moved!

(Wolves jump up and point at the sky.)

WOLVES #2-6: What, huh, where, didyouseeit, what, hey!
WOLF #1: It's Coyote again.

(Wolves look down at ground.)

WOLVES #2-6: *(mumble)* Hey, hi, oh, nothing, nope, nothing, nuh-uh…

COYOTE: Look, fellas, give me a break! I didn't crawl out of the cactus patch yesterday!

WOLF #2: Come on, let's tell Coyote.

WOLF #3: No way! He'll just interfere and mess everything up!

WOLF #4: No, he won't! He's our cousin!

WOLF #5: Coyote always interferes! It's his nature!

WOLF #6: Aw, what the heck! We might as well tell him.

COYOTE: Tell me what?

WOLF #1: Look up in the sky.

COYOTE: I'm looking.

WOLF #2: Do you see those two animals?

COYOTE: Animals? What animals?

WOLF #3: There, in the northern sky!

COYOTE: Oh, *those* animals! What are they?

WOLF #4: We don't know. That's why we're looking at them.

COYOTE: And that's why you're swimming in the shallow end of the gene pool! Are you wolves crazy? If you want to know what kind of animals they are, why don't you just go *up* there and *look*?

WOLF #5: Could we do that?

WOLF #6: I guess we could. See, I said telling Coyote was a good idea.

WOLVES #1-5: *(mumble)* Yeh, right, me, too, sure, uh-uh…

(Wolves stand around without moving.)

COYOTE: So are you guys going up there or what?

WOLVES #1-6: *(mumble)* Yeh, right, sure, sounds good, uh-uh…

WOLF #1: How do we get up there?

COYOTE: Easy. No problem at all.

WOLF #2: Really?

(Coyote takes bow and mimes aiming an arrow at boulder.)

COYOTE: I'll just shoot these arrows into the sky — like so. *(mimes shooting arrow; SOUND: twang or boing noise offstage)* See? Stuck right in there! *(mimes shooting arrow; SOUND: twang or boing noise offstage)* There's another one!

WOLF #3: They'll make a ladder that reaches down to earth!
WOLF #4: And we can climb right up and check out those two animals!

(Wolves cheer.)

WOLF #5: Follow me!
WOLF #6: I'm second!

(As Coyote continues to shoot arrows [with continuing sound effects], Wolves dance counterclockwise around stage from left to right, arriving at boulder just as TWO BEARS step out from behind it. Wolves and Bears are standing to form Big Dipper.)

WOLVES #1-6: Whoa! *(jumping back)* Bears!
COYOTE: Don't go near those Bears! They will tear you to pieces!

(Bears and Wolves regard each other curiously as Coyote cautiously moves up left to get a closer look.)

WOLF #1: They are definitely Bears.
WOLF #2: Oh, definitely, definitely.
WOLF #3: They don't look so terrible!
WOLF #4: Not as terrible as us wolves, eh? Ha-ha-ha!

WOLF #5: Come on, let's relax and shake paws! *(offers hand to Bear #1, who steps forward and shakes it)*

WOLF #6: Hey, Coyote, come over and meet the Bears!

COYOTE: Hmmm. I don't know about that. But you all make a really pretty picture standing together. I think I'll just leave it that way.

(Coyote backs up toward down center and mimes taking arrows out of the sky.)

BEAR #1: Say, what's that Coyote doing?

BEAR #2: He's taking the arrows out of the sky!

WOLF #1: Oh, that's nice. *(double-takes)* He's what?

WOLF #2: Hey, how will we get down?

COYOTE: You won't!

WOLF #3: We'll be stuck up here forever!

COYOTE: That's the idea, cousins!

WOLF #4: Coyote, stop taking the arrows!

WOLF #5: I told you Coyote would interfere!

WOLF #6: Coyote, stop!

NARRATOR: But Coyote didn't stop. He took all the arrows out of the sky, and the Wolves and Bears were stuck where they stood forever. You can still see them today. It's a constellation, or group of stars, called "The Big Dipper." In Latin it's called "Ursa Major" — or "Great Bear."

COYOTE: Gee, that was fun! I think I'll go place some more stars! *(exits left)*

NARRATOR: And Coyote tricked other animals into climbing up into the sky, where they were turned into stars, and he arranged *them* in pictures — Crow and Scorpion and Whale and Lizard became the constellations Corvus and Scorpius and Cetus and Lacerta.

(HOUSE LIGHTS FADE OUT. TWINKLING LIGHTS UP THROUGHOUT STAGE AND ON CEILING.)

NARRATOR: And when Coyote was finished, he called Meadowlark over and said:

COYOTE: *(o.s.)* When I am gone, tell all the People it was Coyote who placed the stars!

(Entire Cast comes onstage and sings. MUSIC: "Twinkle, Twinkle, Little Star.")

ALL CHARACTERS: *(sing)*
Twinkle, twinkle, little star,
How I wonder what you are!
Up above the world so high
Like a diamond in the sky.
Twinkle, twinkle, little star;
How I wonder what you are!

(LIGHTS OUT.)

THE END

Twinkle, Twinkle, Little Star
(traditional, arranged by L.E. McCullough)

East of the Sun, West of the Moon

This tale from Norway is a variant of the *Beauty and the Beast* legend, known throughout the world but first published in France in 1757 by Madame Leprince de Beaumont. In this legend cycle, a Prince — held captive as an animal by a witch's spell — can have his humanity restored only by the love and devotion of a woman, usually the youngest daughter of a poor family. A central element in the story is the age-old belief in the power of witches to transform and subvert the natural order through charms and spells, most frequently by changing people into beasts (see also *The Odyssey* in which Circe turns Ulysses' men into swine).

RUNNING TIME: 25 minutes

PLACE: Norway

CAST: 18 actors, min. 2 boys, 9 girls

Father	Mother
White Bear/Prince	Paulina
6 Children	3 Old Women
North Wind	Long-Nose, the Witch
3 Witches	

STAGE SET: table and 2 chairs at down left; table and bench at down right; scrim at mid center

PROPS: top hat, kite, fruit bowl, pear, knapsack, golden apple, golden carding-comb, golden wheel, movable chair with rollers, laundry tub, scrub brush, 2 identical shirts — one white, the other black

EFFECTS: Sound — wind whistling

MUSIC: *We Are a Family*; *I Wonder What's the Mystery*; *East of the Sun, West of the Moon*; *One Little Thing*

COSTUMES: Humans and Witches wear simple medieval peasant clothes; Witches have hideous face masks; White Bear wears bear mask and body covering; North Wind has ribbons or sashes streaming behind him that function as reins

PERFORMANCE NOTE: when goblins, witches, trolls, etc. "burst apart" or die from rays of the sun or magic swords and so forth, they can fling confetti in the air to symbolize their dissolution into smithereens

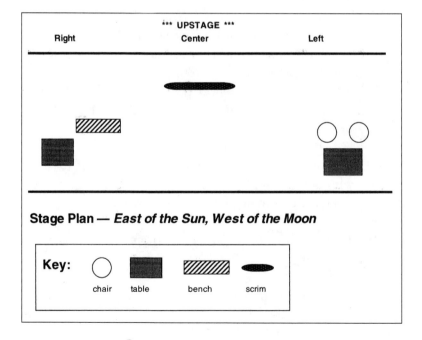

Stage Plan — *East of the Sun, West of the Moon*

(LIGHTS UP FULL; at down left a family gathers around a table and two chairs — MOTHER, FATHER, SIX CHILDREN and PAULINA — with Mother and Father sitting in the chairs and the others gathered around on the floor. MUSIC: "We Are a Family.")

FATHER, MOTHER, SIX CHILDREN & PAULINA: *(sing)*
    Oh, we are a family, a family so poor;
    Of children and babies we have a full score.
    One autumn evening while sitting at tea,
    There came a knock-knocking — one, two and three!

(A WHITE BEAR enters from right and crosses to down center.)

WHITE BEAR: Knock, knock, knock!
MOTHER: Father, please answer the door!
FATHER: I will not! It might be another child trying to enter the house! We have too many already!
WHITE BEAR: Knock, knock, knock!
MOTHER: Father, please answer the door!
FATHER: I will not! It might be another child trying to enter the house! We have too many already!
WHITE BEAR: Knock, knock, knock!
MOTHER: Father, if you won't answer the door, at least go see who is knocking!
FATHER: That I can manage!

(Father gets up and crosses to down center; he peers out the door.)

FATHER: It appears to be a bear!
SIX CHILDREN: A bear!
MOTHER: What sort of a bear?
FATHER: It appears to be a white bear!
SIX CHILDREN: A white bear!

MOTHER: What sort of a white bear?

FATHER: It appears to be a white bear with a top hat and kite!

SIX CHILDREN: A white bear with a top hat and kite!

MOTHER: Fiddlesticks! I've never heard of a such a sight! Open the door!

(Father mimes opening door; White Bear enters and takes off his hat.)

WHITE BEAR: Good evening, all!

FATHER: The same to you!

MOTHER & SIX CHILDREN: The same to you!

FATHER: Would you care for tea?

MOTHER: Perhaps a snack?

FATHER: We haven't much—

MOTHER: But you're welcome to that.

WHITE BEAR: I ask one favor.

FATHER: He asks one favor.

MOTHER: What is that favor.

FATHER: Ask any favor.

MOTHER: Please, name your favor?

WHITE BEAR: Give me your youngest daughter.

(Pause, as Father and Mother and Six Children look at Paulina.)

FATHER, MOTHER & SIX CHILDREN: *(point to Paulina)* Paulina?

WHITE BEAR: If that be her name.

FATHER: That's rather direct!

MOTHER: That's rather strange!

FATHER: That's rather odd!

MOTHER: I think he's deranged!

WHITE BEAR: If you give me your youngest daughter, I will make you as rich tomorrow as you are poor today.

(Pause, as Father and Mother and Six Children look at Paulina.)

FATHER: No, we really couldn't!

MOTHER: No, we really can't!

SIX CHILDREN: After all, she *is* our sister — not some potted plant!

PAULINA: But if I can end our poverty, I will gladly leave with haste.

FATHER: Then pack your bags, Paulina dear; there's not a second left to waste!

(White Bear puts his hat back on and takes Paulina by the arm; with his other arm he holds the kite above their heads; they cross to down right as the family waves goodbye. MUSIC: "We Are a Family.")

FATHER, MOTHER & SIX CHILDREN: *(sing)*
Oh farewell, dear daughter, dear sister, dear gal;
We hope you'll enjoy your white furry pal.
He's big and he's mighty, with teeth three feet long;
Perhaps when he eats you, he'll sing you a song.

(Father, Mother and Six Children exit left; White Bear and Paulina stand at down right.)

PAULINA: This is a wonderful castle. Why, every room is gleaming with gold and silver! And this table is filled with the most delightful things to eat!

WHITE BEAR: I am sure you will enjoy your stay. You have only to ask and anything you desire will be brought to you on command.

PAULINA: You are very generous.

WHITE BEAR: But there is one thing…

PAULINA: Yes?

WHITE BEAR: You must give me your word... you will never
  go into the room next door.
PAULINA: Never?
WHITE BEAR: Never!
PAULINA: I think that is quite clear.
WHITE BEAR: Never! Never!
PAULINA: I will obey, have no fear.
WHITE BEAR: Never! Never!
PAULINA: I won't even come near.
WHITE BEAR: Never! Never!
PAULINA: You have my word most sincere!

(*White Bear exits right; Paulina picks a pear from fruit
bowl, then sits on bench, looking bored. MUSIC: "I
Wonder What's the Mystery."*)

PAULINA: (*sings*)
  I have been in this castle now for ten months;
  And not a single human being in sight.
  Yet in this room next to my room,
  There is someone who sleeps at night.

  I wonder what's the mystery?
  I wonder what's the game?
  I wonder what the purpose is?
  Why won't someone explain?

(*Paulina stands and walks slowly to the scrim at mid
center.*)

PAULINA: (*sings*)
  I suppose I am well-treated;
  I want for nothing at all.
  But I must know who's snoring
  On the other side of the wall!

I wonder what's the mystery?
I wonder what's to hide?
I wonder what the puzzle is?
I'll take a peek inside!

(Paulina slowly lifts the scrim aside and stifles a scream.)

PAULINA: Ohhh!

(She drops the scrim and runs a few feet to the right, covering her face with her hands; a PRINCE emerges from the scrim and approaches her angrily.)

PRINCE: Alas! What have you done, Paulina?
PAULINA: Who are you? How do you know my name?
PRINCE: I am a prince upon whom an evil witch has cast a spell. During the days I appear as a white bear. Only at night do I resume my form as a man.
PAULINA: How can the spell be broken?
PRINCE: By finding a love who would be faithful to her word for one full year. Another two months, Paulina, and you would have saved me from the witch! For now I must go to the castle that lies East of the Sun, West of the Moon.
PAULINA: Is it a nice castle?
PRINCE: I've seen worse.
PAULINA: Then let us go!
PRINCE: You cannot go with me. Long-Nose the Witch lives there. And I am now bound to marry her!

(Prince takes Paulina by the hand, and they walk to down center. MUSIC: "East of the Sun, West of the Moon.")

PRINCE: *(sings)*
From the moment we first met each other,

Cruel fate has kept us apart.
Someday our hearts will be singing in tune
East of the Sun, West of the Moon.

PAULINA: *(sings)*
I see in your eyes a true kindness
That time cannot take away.
Somehow our hearts will rendezvous soon
East of the Sun, West of the Moon.

PRINCE & PAULINA: *(sing)*
For no matter how far we must travel,
No matter the hardships we bear,
We'll meet again, be it cave or cocoon
East of the Sun, West of the Moon.
East of the Sun, West of the Moon.

(Prince exits left; Paulina stands for several seconds with head bowed at center, then perks up.)

PAULINA: Well, I am going to find that witch's castle and break that spell on the Prince!

(OLD WOMAN #1 hobbles out from right; Paulina greets her.)

PAULINA: Ah, here is an old woman. I bet she has much wisdom. I beg your pardon, madame. Do you know the way to the castle that lies East of the Sun, West of the Moon?
OLD WOMAN #1: It is hither and thither, but I know not where. You might ask my neighbor further down the road.
PAULINA: Thank you, madame.

(Old Woman #1, carrying a knapsack, starts hobbling to exit left, then stops.)

OLD WOMAN #1: Oh, and take this golden apple. It might prove useful on your journey.

(Paulina takes the apple and the Old Woman's knapsack and marvels at the apple as Old Woman #1 exits left.)

PAULINA: Apple, apple bright and gold, how can I find my Prince so bold? *(puts apple in knapsack)*

(OLD WOMAN #2 hobbles out from right; Paulina greets her.)

PAULINA: I beg your pardon, madame. Do you know the way to the castle that lies East of the Sun, West of the Moon?
OLD WOMAN #2: It is hither and thither, but I know not where. You might ask my neighbor further down the road.
PAULINA: Thank you, madame.

(Old Woman #2 starts hobbling to exit left, then stops.)

OLD WOMAN #2: Oh, and take this golden carding-comb. It might prove useful on your journey.

(Paulina takes the carding-comb and marvels at it as Old Woman #2 exits left.)

PAULINA: Comb that glitters, won't you speak? And lead me to the castle I seek? *(puts carding-comb in knapsack)*

(OLD WOMAN #3 hobbles out from right; Paulina greets her.)

PAULINA: Madame, I have been traveling for days. Do you

know the way to the castle that lies East of the Sun, West of the Moon?

OLD WOMAN #3: It is hither and thither, but I know not where. You might ask the North Wind to carry you there.

PAULINA: The North Wind? Why, of course! Thank you, madame.

(Old Woman #3 starts hobbling to exit left, then stops.)

OLD WOMAN #3: Oh, and take this golden spinning wheel. It might prove useful on your journey.

(Paulina takes the wheel and marvels at it as Old Woman #3 exits left.)

PAULINA: Wheel of weather, wheel of woe, tell me where the North Wind blows! *(puts spinning wheel in knapsack, puts knapsack on her back)*

(SOUND: wind whistling loudly offstage. NORTH WIND enters from right and strides to down center. Wind noise fades out.)

NORTH WIND: *I* am the North Wind! Who summons me?

PAULINA: I, Paulina, who searches for the castle that lies East of the Sun, West of the Moon. Can you take me there?

NORTH WIND: *I* am the North Wind! I can take you *anywhere!* But I must warn you — it is very long, hard ride. Won't a mere human like you be afraid?

PAULINA: I *will* be afraid. But I will not let my fear stop me from doing what I must. Please take me there right away!

NORTH WIND: Very well. Come along and hold on tight!

(North Wind swirls his streamers, as Paulina grabs hold of one or two of the sashes on his back. SOUND:

wind whistling loudly offstage. North Wind and Paulina whirl around stage once or twice, before Paulina lets go and stops at mid center in front of scrim and North Wind exits right.)

PAULINA: At last! I have found the castle that lies East of the Sun, West of the Moon! It is just turning dark, and no one seems to be at home. I shall spend the night playing with my apple.

(Paulina lays down the knapsack a few feet in front of the scrim, takes out the golden apple and tosses it in the air once or twice; LONG-NOSE THE WITCH peeks out from behind the scrim.)

LONG-NOSE: Who are you?
PAULINA: My name is Paulina. Are you Lady Long-Nose?
LONG-NOSE: I am the Witch Long-Nose, soon to be Princess Long-Nose. I have no time for peddlers! Begone or I'll turn you into a toad!
PAULINA: Then you won't get to know the secret of my golden apple.
LONG-NOSE: Hmmm. What price are you asking for your apple?
PAULINA: It is not for sale. But I will give it to you for nothing if I may see the Prince.
LONG-NOSE: *(cackles)* Hee-hee-hee-hee! You want to see the Prince, eh? So does every young woman, but it won't do you any good because he's going to marry me! Still, give me that apple, and you can see him.

(Long-Nose takes the apple from Paulina and ducks behind the scrim.)

LONG-NOSE: One moment! I'll tell him he has a visitor!

(Long-Nose wheels the Prince out from behind the scrim; he is in a chair and fast asleep. Paulina tries to wake him but cannot.)

PAULINA: Prince! Prince, you must awake! It is I, Paulina!

LONG-NOSE: As you can see, he is fast asleep. It must have something to do with that sleeping potion I mixed in with his bedtime snack. *(cackles)* Hee-hee-hee-hee! Go on, you silly girl! Get away, or I'll turn your elbows inside out!

(Long-Nose wheels the Prince back behind the scrim as Paulina waves goodbye; Paulina goes to her knapsack, takes out the golden carding-comb and examines it.)

PAULINA: Nightfall again and no one about. At least I have this lovely golden carding-comb to amuse me.

(Long-Nose peeks out from behind the scrim.)

LONG-NOSE: You there. What price are you asking for your carding-comb?

PAULINA: It is not for sale. But I will give it to you for nothing if I may see the Prince.

LONG-NOSE: Give me that carding-comb, and you may.

(Long-Nose takes the carding-comb from Paulina and ducks behind the scrim.)

LONG-NOSE: He'll be out in a jiffy!

(Long-Nose wheels the Prince out from behind the scrim; he is again fast asleep. Paulina tries to wake him but cannot.)

PAULINA: Prince! Prince, you must awake! It is I, Paulina!

LONG-NOSE: I'm so sorry, the Prince seems to be otherwise

occupied. *(cackles)* Hee-hee-hee-hee! Get away, now, or I'll make mice come out of your ears!

(Long-Nose wheels the Prince back behind the scrim as Paulina waves goodbye; Paulina goes to her knapsack, takes out the golden spinning wheel and gives it a spin.)

PAULINA: Another night in this lonely place. At least I have still have this lovely golden spinning wheel.

(Long-Nose peeks out from behind the scrim.)

LONG-NOSE: You there. I want that golden spinning wheel. How much do you want for it?
PAULINA: Not a cent, if you let me see the Prince one more time.
LONG-NOSE: Done.

(Long-Nose takes the spinning wheel from Paulina and ducks behind the scrim.)

LONG-NOSE: Make way for the royal bridegroom!

(Long-Nose wheels the Prince out from behind the scrim; he is again fast asleep. Paulina tries to wake him but cannot.)

PAULINA: Prince! Prince, you must awake! It is I, Paulina!
LONG-NOSE: *(cackles)* Hee-hee-hee-hee! This is better than taking candy from a baby! Oh, I've got to tell the other witches! Hee-hee-hee-hee! *(goes behind scrim)*
PAULINA: *(kneels beside Prince)* My poor Prince, I have traveled so far to find you! But, alas, all is lost! I cannot release you from your spell!
PRINCE: *(opens his eyes)* Yes, you can.

PAULINA: *(startled)* Aii! You are awake?

PRINCE: Sshhh! When Long-Nose gave me the drink with the sleeping potion tonight, I secretly poured it out. But listen — we have little time, for the wedding is planned for tomorrow at midnight.

PAULINA: Midnight!

PRINCE: Yes. Witches can never abide the daylight. When the sun sets tomorrow, be waiting at the castle gate. *(closes eyes and feigns sleep)*

(Long-Nose comes out and wheels the Prince back behind the scrim as Paulina waves goodbye.)

LONG-NOSE: Have a nice chat, dearie? Hee-hee-hee-hee! Not much of a talker, is he? Hee-hee-hee-hee! I think a witch has got his tongue! Hee-hee-hee-hee!

PAULINA: Not for long, I predict.

(Paulina walks to down center and sings. MUSIC: "East of the Sun, West of the Moon.")

PAULINA: *(sings)*
For no matter how far we must travel,
No matter the hardships we bear,
We'll meet again, be it cave or cocoon
East of the Sun, West of the Moon.

(Paulina sits facing audience and puts her head on her knees. LIGHTS OUT FOR FIVE SECONDS, THEN UP FULL.)

PAULINA: *(awakes with a start, gazes upward)* The moon rises and stars sprinkle the sky! It is the Prince's wedding night!

(The Prince strides out from behind scrim, holding a white shirt, with Long-Nose behind him.)

PRINCE: My wedding night, and you expect me to wear a shirt with a stain? Before I marry, I will see what my bride can do with a laundry brush! *(shoves shirt at Long-Nose)*

LONG-NOSE: *(takes shirt)* You are troubled by a mere stain? *(sniffs shirt)* Hmmm… smells like Sleeping Potion Number Nine! I wonder how that got on this shirt?

PRINCE: Never you mind! That shirt must be clean before I marry!

LONG-NOSE: Witches! Bring me the cauldron!

(THREE WITCHES enter from left and roll out laundry tub to mid center. Long-Nose takes shirt and puts it in tub.)

LONG-NOSE: And where is the scrub brush?

(Witch #1 hands her a scrub brush.)

WITCH #1: Sorry.

LONG-NOSE: May your rabbits have kittens!

(Long-Nose scrubs, stops and looks at shirt, then scowls. She scrubs harder, stops and looks again, scowls again.)

PRINCE: *(impatiently)* And how is my shirt coming along?

LONG-NOSE: *(scrubs even harder)* Fine, fine, everything is fine!

(Prince approaches to look.)

LONG-NOSE: No peeking, now! Everything... is... just... fine!

(Long-Nose slumps over tub, exhausted. Witch #2 holds up black shirt.)

PRINCE: By the great horn spoon, you've turned my wedding shirt black! I won't be marrying you, Lady Long-Nose! Who else wants to give it a try?

WITCH #1: I do! I do!

WITCH #2: My turn!

WITCH #3: Me! Me! Me!

(Witch #2 seizes scrub brush from Long-Nose, dips shirt into tub and begins scrubbing vigorously. MUSIC: "One Little Thing." Throughout song, Witches #1 and #3 take turns scrubbing with Witch #2.)

WITCH #1, 2 & 3: *(sing)*
We're witches! We're witches!
We can do so many things!
We turn puppies into bullfrogs,
We make teacups dance and sing!

We're witches! We're witches!
We're powerful and mean!
But the one little thing we cannot do
Is get this wedding shirt clean!

LONG-NOSE: *(sings)*
Once I put a lovely spell on the king and queen of France;
I turned them into wiggly worms and, curiously, by chance,
They were used as bait to hook the biggest snail in all Paree,
And ended up as fresh hors d'oeuvres at the afternoon tea!

WITCH #1, 2 & 3: *(sing)*
> We're witches! We're witches!
> We can do so many things!
> We turn puppies into bullfrogs,
> We make teacups dance and sing!
>
> We're witches! We're witches!
> We're powerful and mean!
> But the one little thing we cannot do
> Is get this wedding shirt clean!

LONG-NOSE: *(sings)*
> I can put a gruesome spell on any fool who bothers me;
> I can turn a charging knight into a weeping willow tree.
> My curses and enchantments can stop the tracks of time;
> There is no earthly limit to the compass of my crime!

WITCH #1, 2 & 3: *(sing)*
> Because we're witches! We're witches!
> We can do so many things!
> We turn puppies into bullfrogs,
> We make teacups dance and sing!
>
> We're witches! We're witches!
> We're powerful and mean!
> But the one little thing we cannot do
> Is get this wedding shirt clean!

(Prince strolls over to tub.)

PRINCE: Every witch in the woods has spent hours trying to clean my wedding shirt. Let us see the result.

(Prince lifts up black shirt and sighs.)

WITCHES #1, 2 & 3: Well, if we can't do it, nobody can!
PRINCE: I am not so certain of that. Why, there is someone

standing by the castle gate. I say, young lass! Would you take a turn at washing my wedding shirt?

PAULINA: Thank you very much.

(Paulina takes the black shirt and dips it into tub.)

LONG-NOSE: Hah! She has no spells or magic powers! What can she do to the wedding shirt that we could not?

(Paulina takes the white shirt out and holds it up; Witches and Long-Nose gasp.)

PAULINA: *I* can get it clean!
PRINCE: And thus will be my bride!
WITCH #1: How did she do that?
WITCH #2: She probably has a pure, clean heart.
WITCH #3: Let's cut it out and see for ourselves!

(Long-Nose confronts Prince and Paulina, Witches gathered behind her in threatening pose.)

LONG-NOSE: Foolish mortals! Prepare to meet your eternal doom!
PRINCE: No, foul witches! Prepare to meet yours! *(points upward)* See, the sun rises!
PAULINA: The witches are melted by the fiery fingers of the dawn!
PRINCE: And we are free, Paulina, from the spell of Long-Nose!

(SPOTLIGHT ON Long-Nose and Witches, who crumple to floor, moaning and screaming.)

LONG-NOSE & WITCHES: Aiieeee! We're mellllllllting! Aiieeee!

(Long-Nose and Witches die; SPOTLIGHT FOLLOWS Prince and Paulina as they walk to down center. North Wind enters from right.)

PAULINA: Why, look! It is the North Wind!

NORTH WIND: Last call back to Norseland. Allllll aboard the North Wind Express!

(Prince and Paulina take hold of North Wind's streamers; they sing. MUSIC: "East of the Sun, West of the Moon.")

PRINCE: *(sings)*
From the moment we first met each other,

PAULINA: *(sings)*
Our wedding was never in doubt.

PRINCE & PAULINA: *(sing)*
This is the day our hearts sing in tune
East of the Sun, West of the Moon.
East of the Sun, West of the Moon.

(Entire Cast gathers at center stage and sings. MUSIC: "We Are a Family.")

ENTIRE CAST: *(sing)*
Oh, we are a family of melody and rhyme;
Of witches and goblins and wizards sublime.
You've heard our fairy tale, now join in our tune;
Sing East of the Sun, sing West of the Moon.

(LIGHTS OUT.)

THE END

We Are a Family
(words & music by L.E. McCullough)

♩ = 150

G
Oh, we are a fa- mi- ly, a **C** fa- mi- ly so

G
poor; of chil- dren and ba- bies we **C** **G** have a full

D **C**
score. One au- tumn **G** e- ven- ing while sit- **C** ting at

Em **G**
tea; there came a **D** knock- knock- ing — **C** one, two and **G** three!

© L.E. McCullough 1997

East of the Sun, West of the Moon

(words & music by L.E. McCullough)

♩ = 120

From the mo- ment we first met each o- ther, cruel fate has kept us a- part. Some- day our hearts will be sing- ing in tune, East of the Sun, West of the Moon.

I Wonder What's the Mystery
(words & music by L.E. McCullough)

♩ = 105

I have been in this cas- tle now for ten months; and

not a sin- gle hu- man being in sight. Yet in this room next to

my room, there is some- one who sleeps at night. I

won- der what's the mys-te- ry? I won- der what's the game? I

won- der what the pur- pose is? Why won't some- one ex- plain?

One Little Thing
(words & music by L.E. McCullough)

We're wit- ches! We're wit- ches! We can do so ma- ny things! We turn

pupp- ies in- to bull- frogs, we make tea- cups dance and sing! We're

wit- ches! We're wit- ches! We're pow- er- ful and mean! But the

one lit- tle thing we can- not do is get this wed- ding shirt

(Verse 1)

clean! Once I put a love- ly spell on the

king and queen of France; I turned them in- to

One Little Thing, pg. 2

Gm   Cm   Fm

wig- gly worms and, cur- i- ous- ly, by chance, They were

Cm   Fm Cm

used to bait the big- gest snail in all Pa- ree, and end- ed

Fm   Gm   *D.C.*

up as fresh hors d'oeuvres at the af- ter- noon tea! We're

(Verse 2) Cm   Gm   Cm

I can put a grue- some spell on a- ny fool who both- ers

Gm   Cm

me; I can turn a char- ging knight in-

Fm   Cm   Fm

to a weep- ing wil- low tree. My cur- ses and en- chant-ments can

Cm   Fm

stop the tracks of time; There is no earth- ly li- mit to the

Gm   C   *D.C.*

© L.E. McCullough 1997

com- pass of my crime! Be- cause we're

The Great Flying Ship of Ivan the Impossible

This Russian fairy tale has all the elements of the standard "tall tale" that would become a staple of American folklore during the 19th century — ordinary people performing extraordinary feats of strength and skill in a humorous manner. A German nobleman, Baron von Munchausen (1720-1797), is credited with popularizing this type of far-fetched "whopper" by exaggerating his adventures serving in the Russian army against the Turks. The plot in this play belongs to the "son-in-law test" cycle of tales, in which a young man wishing to marry a king or rich man's daughter must accomplish seemingly impossible tasks in a short time. Not as hard as it looks, when you have the sort of friends Ivan the Impossible did!

RUNNING TIME: 20 minutes

PLACE: Russia

CAST: 17 actors, min. 4 boys, 2 girls

Ivan the Impossible	Old Man
Ivan's Mother	Sharp Ear
Ivan's Father	Swift Foot
Tsar	Hawk Eye
Tsarina	Hay Maker
2 Tsar's Servants	Wood Cutter
4 Soldiers	

STAGE SET: 2 stools at down right; a bench at down left; scrim or backdrop painting of ship wheeled in at mid center

PROPS: ping-pong ball, letter, sandwich, knapsack, bow, bundle of kindling, bundle of straw, banana, golden candlestick, a large cardboard box or plastic tub, bath towel

EFFECTS: Sound — wind whistling; bow *boing* or *twang*

MUSIC: *A Ship with Wings; Good Friends Appreciate*

COSTUMES: Ivan the Impossible, Ivan's Mother, Ivan's Father, Old Man and Ivan's friends wear simple medieval peasant clothes; Sharp Ear might have a large cardboard ear; Hawk Eye a small telescope, Swift Foot a pair of oversized shoes or boots, Hay Maker a small pronged trowel, Wood Cutter a small axe; Tsar and Tsarina wear royal garb with crowns; Soldiers wear 17th/18th-century shako-style hats with feathers and carry swords or spears; Servants dress as medieval pages

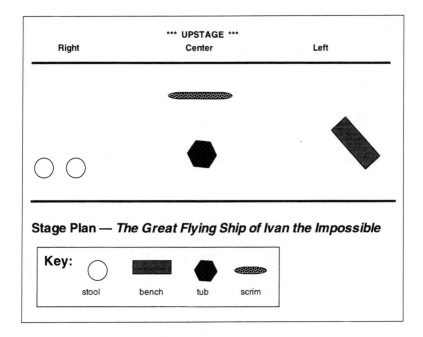

Stage Plan — *The Great Flying Ship of Ivan the Impossible*

Key: stool   bench   tub   scrim

(LIGHTS UP FULL on IVAN'S MOTHER and IVAN'S FATHER at down right; Ivan's Mother and Ivan's Father sit on stools. IVAN THE IMPOSSIBLE stands at down center, giggling and trying to balance a ping-pong ball on the end of his nose.)

IVAN'S MOTHER: *(to audience)* Once upon time—

IVAN'S FATHER: A very long time ago—

IVAN'S MOTHER: A little family lived in the middle of the vast steppes of Russia.

IVAN'S FATHER: She is talking about us, you know.

IVAN'S MOTHER: There was a mother.

IVAN'S FATHER: And a father, don't forget.

IVAN'S MOTHER: Who had a son, Ivan. Who they affectionately nicknamed—

IVAN'S FATHER: "Ivan the Impossible"!

IVAN: Mother, father, look! I can balance a ball on the end of my nose! *(drops ball, giggles)* Almost! Hee-hee!

IVAN'S FATHER: Ay-yi-yi! Ivan, you are impossible!

IVAN'S MOTHER: Ivan has always been a little bit "different" than other children.

IVAN'S FATHER: A little *too* different, I say. Look at him there, trying to balance that silly ball on his nose. What will he be when he grows up? A clown in a circus?

IVAN'S MOTHER: He's just very sensitive, that's all. You shouldn't be criticizing him all the time. You'll give him a complex!

IVAN'S FATHER: Better a complex than a kick in the pants! I tried teaching him to plow and to tend crops and to shoe horses, but he won't learn! He sits around all day doing crazy things! He's — *impossible!*

(Ivan tries to stuff ball into his ear.)

IVAN: Mother, father, I can't get this ball to go in my ear! Owww! Ow-ow-ow-ow-ow!

IVAN'S FATHER: Ay-yi-yi! I give up!

IVAN'S MOTHER: *(produces letter)* One day a letter from the Tsar was sent to every village in Russia. *(reads)* "Whatever boy or man builds a ship that can fly, to him I will give my daughter, the Tsarina, in marriage."

IVAN: That sounds like fun! I think I'll go build a ship that can fly!

(Ivan sings. MUSIC: "A Ship with Wings.")

IVAN: (SINGS)
If I could build a ship with wings,
I'd fly the world round!
I'd sail above the wispy clouds
Miles above the ground!

I'd soar above the people who
Say that I'm a fool.
I'd prove to them my valor
With deeds both brave and true.

IVAN'S MOTHER: *(to Ivan's Father)* Dear, don't let him go! It's liable to be very dangerous!

IVAN'S FATHER: Of course it's liable to be dangerous!

IVAN'S MOTHER: But he's liable to get into harm!

IVAN'S FATHER: Of course he's liable to get into harm!

IVAN'S MOTHER: But he's liable to never return!

IVAN'S FATHER: So what's your point? Let the boy go already before he sings another song! Besides, it is his destiny!

IVAN'S MOTHER: Ivan received a final gift from his parents.

IVAN'S FATHER: Here, take a ham sandwich. *(hands Ivan a sandwich that Ivan stuffs in his knapsack)* You never know when it might come in handy.

IVAN: To eat when I'm hungry?

IVAN'S FATHER: No, to ride when you're tired of walking!

Ay-yi-yi! Ivan, you are truly impossible! Now go on, get out of here!

IVAN'S MOTHER: And Ivan went on his way to attempt the most impossible thing in the world.

(Ivan's Mother and Ivan's Father exit right; Ivan walks around the stage; an OLD MAN hobbles onstage from left and pauses at down left, where Ivan hails him.)

IVAN: Greetings, aged one!

OLD MAN: Good day to you, my son. To where are you travelling?

IVAN: To wherever I can find a ship that will fly. Have you seen one?

OLD MAN: No. But rest awhile here. *(sits on bench)* Will you share with me the food in your knapsack?

IVAN: Good sir, I would gladly share it with you, but you wouldn't want it. It is merely a ham sandwich my father says to ride when I'm tired of walking.

OLD MAN: Nonsense! Take it out! Any blessing of food from the Almighty is good enough to eat!

(Ivan reaches into knapsack and is greatly surprised.)

IVAN: This is impossible! Instead of a single ham sandwich, there is an entire banquet of savory meats and fruits!

OLD MAN: Not as impossible as you might think. *(points to mid center)* Go now to the woods there, straight up to the first tree.

(Ivan goes to mid center.)

OLD MAN: Take your ham sandwich and give the tree one blow.

(Ivan mimes striking a tree trunk with sandwich.)

OLD MAN: Then lie down and sleep for one hour. You will have your flying ship and may proceed on your travels. But whoever you meet along the way, you must invite into your ship.

(Ivan lies down face-first; a scrim or backdrop painting of ship can be wheeled or moved up behind him; LIGHTS FADE DOWN THEN UP as Ivan awakes, yawning.)

IVAN: What a pleasant nap… I wonder why I've been sleeping in the woods? *(sees ship and jumps up)* A flying ship! Why, that is impossible! But of course, I *am* Ivan the Impossible!

(Ivan sits on floor facing audience and mimes steering a car and looking down at the ground below. SOUND: wind whistling.)

IVAN: I am flying! I am really flying! Oh, how I wish mother and father could see me now!

(SHARP EAR enters from left and puts his ear to the ground. SOUND STOPS.)

IVAN: Greetings, fellow traveler! Why do you have your ear stuck to the ground?
SHARP EAR: Two friends are talking in Africa. I am listening to their conversation.
IVAN: My word, but you must have very good hearing! Come aboard my flying ship, and we will visit the Tsar in Moscow!

(Sharp Ear sits behind and to the left of Ivan; Ivan steers the ship gleefully. SOUND: wind whistling.)

IVAN: Isn't this fun!

SHARP EAR: A flying ship? It is impossible!

IVAN: It certainly is! And that makes it even more fun!

(SWIFT FOOT enters from left, hopping on one leg. SOUND STOPS.)

IVAN: Say there, good sir! Why are you hopping on one leg? Are you injured?

SWIFT FOOT: Not at all. But, so long are my steps, that if I were to walk with both legs, I would stride across half the world in a second!

IVAN: My flying ship is almost as quick. Come aboard!

(Swift Foot sits behind and to the right of Ivan; Ivan steers the ship gleefully. SOUND: wind whistling.)

IVAN: I have never driven a flying ship before! Nor have I ever had two such good friends!

SWIFT FOOT: We may not talk much…

SHARP EAR: But we sure appreciate the ride!

(SOUND STOPS. They sing. MUSIC: "Good Friends Appreciate.")

SWIFT FOOT: *(sings)*
Good friends appreciate the things we do;
SHARP EAR: *(sings)*
Good friends appreciate the things we like;
SWIFT FOOT & SHARP EAR: *(sing)*
Good friends appreciate who we are,
IVAN: *(sings)*
And make you appreciate you!

SWIFT FOOT, SHARP EAR & IVAN: *(sing)*
Good friends will appreciate you when you're feeling low;
Good friends never hesitate to help you reach your goal.

SWIFT FOOT: *(sings)*
> Good friends appreciate the things we say;

SHARP EAR: *(sings)*
> Good friends appreciate the things we feel;

SWIFT FOOT & SHARP EAR: *(sing)*
> Good friends appreciate who we are,

IVAN: *(sings)*
> And make you appreciate you, too!

(HAWK EYE enters from left, aiming a bow at offstage right.)

IVAN: *(points)* Look at that archer down on the ground!

SWIFT FOOT: Where is he aiming the bow? Where is the target?

SHARP EAR: I don't know. I can't see a thing.

IVAN: Greetings, bold archer! At what are you aiming?

HAWK EYE: At a pea the size of a pinhead about ten miles down the way.

IVAN: We're going right past there, if you'd like a lift!

HAWK EYE: I would indeed!

(Hawk Eye sits behind Ivan as WOOD CUTTER enters from left carrying a bundle of kindling on his back followed by HAY MAKER carrying a bundle of straw in his arms.)

SHARP EAR: Look, a Wood Cutter!

SWIFT FOOT: And a Hay Maker!

IVAN: Why are they dragging that wood and straw about?

WOOD CUTTER: This is not common wood. It is magic wood.

HAY MAKER: And this is magic straw.

WOOD CUTTER: When I scatter these sticks on the ground, an entire army springs up, ready to take the field!

HAY MAKER: And when I spread this straw upon the ground,

a layer of snow and frost arises, even on the hottest summer day!

IVAN: You two sound like very interesting people. Would you like a ride to Moscow to see the Tsar?

WOOD CUTTER & HAY MAKER: We would like that very much!

IVAN: Then climb aboard!

(Wood Cutter and Hay Maker sit on either side of Hawk Eye. They all sing and steer as if flying. MUSIC: "Good Friends Appreciate.")

ALL: *(sing)*
Good friends appreciate the things we say;
Good friends appreciate the things we feel;
Good friends appreciate who we are,
And make you appreciate you, too!

(TSAR, followed by TWO SERVANTS, enter from left and stand at down left facing right.)

HAWK EYE: *(peers at audience)* I see the spires of Moscow!
SHARP EAR: *(cranes ear)* I hear the footsteps of her people!
SWIFT FOOT: *(points)* There is the Tsar's palace!
WOOD CUTTER: *(points)* There are the Tsar's servants!
HAY MAKER: *(points)* There is the Tsar!

(TSARINA enters from right and stands at down center facing left.)

IVAN: And there is the Tsarina!

(With Ivan in lead, party in ship rise and approach the Tsar; they bow humbly.)

SERVANT #1: He has brought a flying ship!

TSAR: This is impossible! Who is this young man?

IVAN: I am Impossible, sire! *(bows)*

SERVANT #2: Do not mock the Tsar! He asked your name!

IVAN: That *is* my name. I am called Ivan the Impossible! And I have brought you the flying ship you requested.

TSAR: But that is impossible!

IVAN: Indeed, O Tsar, it is. And I am. Ivan the Impossible, that is.

TSARINA: Then you are the man I shall marry!

(Ivan smiles and starts toward Tsarina; Tsar intervenes.)

TSAR: Not so fast, young fellow! We expected someone of noble birth to bring us the flying ship. You are but a peasant.

IVAN: Peasant is as peasant does, sire.

TSAR: Then you must perform a peasant task. Perform it nobly, and—

IVAN: I can marry the Tsarina?

TSAR: Ummmm, we'll talk about it.

SERVANT #1: First, you shall get your master, the Tsar, a golden candlestick—

IVAN: No problem.

SERVANT #2: From the other end of the world—

IVAN: Still no problem.

SERVANT #1: By the time the Tsar finishes eating this banana.

(Servant #1 hands Tsar a banana.)

IVAN: What! That is impossible!

SERVANT #2: If you fail—

TSAR: You will forfeit your life!

IVAN: Is that absolutely necessary?

SERVANTS #1 & 2: The Tsar has spoken!

(Tsar sits on bench and begins slowly eating the banana; Servants #1 & 2 stand behind him, while the Tsarina sits at his feet.)

SWIFT FOOT: Don't worry, friend Ivan! I know exactly where the golden candlestick is kept. With my amazing speed and stride, I shall bring it back in an instant! *(exits right)*

IVAN: *(waves farewell to Swift Foot)* Godspeed, friend Swift Foot! Does anyone have a watch?

SHARP EAR: Don't worry, Ivan. Swift Foot is awfully fast.

HAWK EYE: Why, he should have been back by now.

IVAN: I wonder if the Tsar is going to eat the peel? I think the peel should count as part of the banana, don't you?

(Sharp Ear bends down to the floor and listens.)

SHARP EAR: Oh, no! Swift Foot must have lain down to take a nap! I hear him snoring under an oak tree about two thousand miles away!

HAWK EYE: *(aims bow at down right)* Never fear! I will wake him!

(Hawk Eye shoots the arrow. SOUND: bow boing or twang.)

SWIFT FOOT: *(o.s.)* Owww! Whoops, gotta run!

(Swift Foot races onstage from right with golden candlestick, which he gives to Ivan, who presents it to the Tsar just as the Tsar takes the last bite of banana.)

TSAR: Servants, sharpen your swords for the beheading!

IVAN: Here is the golden candlestick, O Tsar!

TSAR: Oh yes, the golden candlestick — what?!? *(chokes on banana)*

IVAN: Now may I marry the Tsarina?

TSAR: I said we'd talk about it.

IVAN: Yes!

TSAR: And we are talking about it.

IVAN: Yes!

TSAR: And the answer is no.

SERVANTS #1 & 2: No!

IVAN: No?

SERVANTS #1 & 2: No!

TSARINA: Father, I am very fond of this young man. After all, he did bring you a flying ship.

(Servants #1 & 2 whisper in Tsar's ears.)

TSAR: My dear Tsarina, if you really desire this young peasant as your husband, I suppose you may marry him. But first, he must take the official wedding bath!

(Servants #1 & 2 go offstage left and bring back a tub, setting it at down center; they turn around to face upstage.)

WOOD CUTTER: Ivan, that tub is made of cast-iron!

HAY MAKER: And the water is heated hotter than hot!

WOOD CUTTER: If you take the official wedding bath—

HAY MAKER: You will be the official wedding lobster!

IVAN: Do you think perhaps the Tsar doesn't like me?

HAY MAKER: Do not worry, friend Ivan. I will solve the problem.

(Hay Maker scatters straw around tub.)

WOOD CUTTER: Hay Maker is scattering his magic straw. See the snow and frost arise!

IVAN: The entire room is turning freezing cold!

HAY MAKER: You may take your bath now. *(dips hand into tub)* The water is just right!

(Ivan steps into tub and smiles; Servants #1 & 2 turn around and see him.)

IVAN: Ahhh… that's nice!

SERVANT #1: Still alive! It is impossible!

IVAN: That's my name — don't wear it out!

SERVANT #2: The Tsar will be very upset!

(Servants #1 & 2 cross to Tsar and whisper in his ears; Wood Cutter and Hay Maker help Ivan out of tub, dry him off with a towel.)

TSARINA: Now can I marry Ivan?

TSAR: *(stands)* Not yet! I have one more test!

IVAN: I hope it's a driving test. I just drove a flying ship all the way from Siberia!

TSAR: You must prove you have the resources to keep the Tsarina in a comfortable state. Before morning, you must produce an army!

IVAN: An entire army?

SHARP EAR: He'll raise an entire army!

IVAN: I will? I mean, I will!

HAWK EYE: And if you refuse to keep your word and let him marry the Tsarina—

SWIFT FOOT: He will conquer your kingdom!

IVAN: That's right. I mean, with your permission, sire!

TSAR: To your task, peasant!

(Tsar sits and Tsar, Servants #1 and 2 and Tsarina nod heads and sleep.)

IVAN: Oh no, I've done it now! I have to raise an entire army by morning! Tsar's don't like being threatened by peasants with armies that don't exist!

WOOD CUTTER: Have you forgotten, friend Ivan, my magic sticks?

HAY MAKER: I think he has, Wood Cutter. Better show him how they work.

(LIGHTS FLICKER as Wood Cutter scatters sticks at down right; FOUR SOLDIERS march out from right.)

WOOD CUTTER: There is your army! Forty thousand of the finest soldiers on foot and horse!
HAY MAKER: Forward, march! To the Tsar!

(Ivan leads Four Soldiers to Tsar, who awakes.)

SERVANT #1: It is a multitude in arms swarming throughout the palace!
SERVANT #2: Such an army could conquer the entire kingdom! You must yield, sire!
TSARINA: Then Ivan and I may be married at last?
TSAR: The wedding will proceed. Servants, bring the finest food and drink for our guests!

(Ivan and Tsarina take hands and cross to down center; Ivan's Mother, Ivan's Father and Old Man enter from right; Entire Cast gathers at center behind Ivan and Tsarina.)

IVAN: My father was right. You never know when a ham sandwich will come in handy.
TSARINA: To eat when you're hungry?
IVAN: No. To build a flying ship when I want to marry a Tsarina!

(Entire Cast sings. MUSIC: "A Ship with Wings — Reprise.")

ENTIRE CAST: *(sings)*
>Ivan the Impossible!
>He built a ship with wings!
>Ivan the Impossible!
>He did impossible things!

>He soared above the people
>Who said he was a fool.
>He proved to them his valor
>With deeds both brave and true.

(LIGHTS OUT.)

THE END

A Ship with Wings
(words & music by L.E. McCullough)

© L.E. McCullough 1997

A Ship with Wings — Reprise
(words & music by L.E. McCullough)

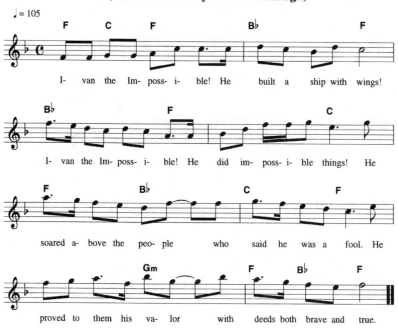

I- van the Im- poss- i- ble! He built a ship with wings!

I- van the Im- poss- i- ble! He did im- poss- i- ble things! He

soared a- bove the peo- ple who said he was a fool. He

proved to them his va- lor with deeds both brave and true.

Good Friends Appreciate
(words & music by L.E. McCullough)

♩ = 125

Good friends a- ppre- ci- ate the things we do;

Good friends a- ppre- ci- ate the things we like;

Good friends a- ppre- ci- ate who we are, and

make you a- ppre- ci- ate you! Good friends will a-

ppre- ci- ate you when you're feel- ing low;

Good friends ne- ver hes- i- tate to help you reach your

Good Friends Appreciate, pg. 2

goal be- cause our Good friends a- ppre- ci- ate the

things we say; Good friends a- ppre- ci- ate the things we feel;

Good friends a- ppre- ci- ate who we are, and

make you a- ppre- ci- ate you, too!

© L.E. McCullough 1997

The Lost Spear

In this tale from West Africa, a peasant boy seeking the hand of his bride must pass a very severe "son-in-law test" — descending into the Land of the Dead to retrieve a lost spear! From the ancient Babylonian story of Ishtar rescuing Tammuz and the Greek myth of Orpheus descending to Hades in search of his wife Eurydice, the saga of a lone warrior courageously facing the lords of the underworld has intrigued storytellers the world over. In *The Lost Spear*, the hero must not only prove his physical prowess but use his intellectual abilities to think his way out of a difficult situation. And, as often occurs in the best fairy tales, he receives timely help from members of the animal kingdom!

RUNNING TIME: 15 minutes

PLACE: Senegal

CAST: 20 actors, min. 5 boys, 2 girls

Griot	King
Zandilli	Princess
3 Suitors	Vulture
Frog	Butterfly
3 Water Lilies	Moon Goddess
3 Fireflies	3 Lizards

STAGE SET: a bench at down left; a throne at mid center

PROPS: spear, brightly-colored cloths, 3 cardboard stacks of water fly wings (sparkly plastic floor mats)

MUSIC: *Call of the Griot*; *Zandilli's Walking Song*; *Sapphire Lake*; *Dance of the Fireflies*

COSTUMES: Humans wear one-piece robes or smocks and sandals; King and Princess have a headdress, feathered necklace and other African jewelry indicating high rank; Animals have appropriate animal masks, wings and body coverings

(LIGHTS UP DOWN RIGHT on GRIOT standing at down right; he addresses audience as vocal chorus sings offstage. MUSIC: "Call of the Griot" — ends with shaking of rattles.)

GRIOT: People of the kingdom, come listen! As chief griot of the royal court of Senegal, my job is to sing praises of kings and queens. To tell the mighty adventures of heroes and heroines. To remember the deeds of our ancestors so that they may inspire us even today. And so it is I now tell the tale of Zandilli and The Lost Spear.

(LIGHTS UP DOWN CENTER AND DOWN LEFT. At down left on a bench sit the KING and PRINCESS. THREE SUITORS and ZANDILLI stand at down center, hands clasped behind their backs, facing audience.)

GRIOT: Long, long ago, there was a King of Senegal who invited the young men of the kingdom to vie in feats of skill for the hand of his daughter, the Princess. On the last day of the contest, there were four suitors left. Three were sons of prominent nobles.

(Three Suitors take a step forward.)

GRIOT: The fourth was the son of a simple herdsman. His name was Zandilli. And, if truth be told, the Princess had already set her heart on having him as her husband, despite his humble birth and station.

(Zandilli steps forward, smiles; Princess half-rises before King sits her down with a scowl.)

KING: Your final challenge is at hand. Whoever throws his spear the farthest, will marry the Princess.

(Suitor #1 mimes throwing a spear into the audience; King claps.)

GRIOT: The first suitor threw his spear about half a mile.

(Suitor #2 mimes throwing a spear into the audience; King claps.)

GRIOT: The second suitor threw his spear more than a mile.

(Suitor #3 mimes throwing a spear into the audience; King claps.)

GRIOT: The third suitor threw his spear nearly two whole miles. But when it was Zandilli's turn —

(Zandilli mimes throwing a spear into the audience; Princess claps, King stops her with a scowl.)

SUITORS #1, 2 & 3: Zandilli has thrown his spear over the mountain into the clouds!

(Suitors #1, 2 & 3 bow down to Zandilli as Princess rushes to Zandilli and kneels beside him.)

SUITORS #1, 2 & 3: Zandilli! Zandilli! Zandilli!

GRIOT: How the people acclaimed their new hero! But the King did not want to give his daughter to the son of a herdsman.

KING: Halt! I believe the spear Zandilli threw was bewitched!

ZANDILLI: That is a lie!

KING: You shall have the Princess only if you find the spear you threw!

PRINCESS: But, father, that is an impossible task! Zandilli's spear flew over the mountain into the clouds!

KING: I am King, and it is for me to decide who you shall marry! *(to Zandilli)* You have seven days to find your spear and bring it back. If you do not, the Princess will be wed to another.

(King exits left, followed by sobbing Princess and Three Suitors; Zandilli wanders upstage left and then right before coming to mid center. MUSIC: "Zandilli's Walking Song.")

GRIOT: Zandilli climbed up the mountain and wandered in the wilds for two days, vainly seeking his spear. On the third day he saw a most curious thing — a Vulture dragging a Frog!

(VULTURE enters from left, dragging FROG toward down center.)

FROG: Please, Vulture, you are making a big mistake! I am not yet dead!

VULTURE: Oh, but you will be soon, my tasty little Frog! Very, very soon! Awwwwk!

ZANDILLI: Wait! *(wrests Frog from Vulture)* Frog is right! You have no business seizing him while he is still alive!

VULTURE: Awwwwk! Mind your own business!

ZANDILLI: *(threatens Vulture with fist)* Go find another poor creature to torment!

VULTURE: Awwwwk! *(stumbles offstage right)*

FROG: You saved my life, and I am forever grateful! If *you* ever need help, just call out these words — "Frog of the forest, Frog of the wood; aid me in my quest for good." I will come to your assistance immediately!

(Frog hops offstage left and Zandilli wanders upstage left and then right before coming to mid center as BUTTERFLY enters from right, twirls to down center and falls to ground, as if caught on a thorn.)

GRIOT: And the Frog dove into the water with a big splash! Zandilli walked on the third day, again without finding his lost spear. On the fourth day he saw another curious sight — a beautiful Butterfly caught on the prickly thorns of a pear bush.

(Zandilli helps free Butterfly.)

BUTTERFLY: Thank you! You are quite gentle for a human! What is your name?

ZANDILLI: My name is Zandilli, son of a plain herdsman.

BUTTERFLY: Your father has taught you well. If *you* ever need help, Zandilli, just call out these words — "Butterfly, butterfly, fluttering free; send your comfort quick to me." I will assist you right away!

(Butterfly twirls offstage left as LIGHTS FADE OUT EXCEPT FOR SPOTLIGHT ON Zandilli standing at down center.)

GRIOT: Zandilli walked on and very soon came to a cave. At the entrance he heard music. It was the most beautiful music he had ever heard.

(Opening bars of "Sapphire Lake" played as instrumental offstage; Zandilli turns and moves slowly up right, followed by SPOTLIGHT.)

GRIOT: Zandilli entered the cave, boldly following the music. The music grew louder with each step, and suddenly Zandilli found himself standing on the shore of a sapphire lake!

(LIGHTS UP FULL on THREE WATER LILLIES dancing at left center and MOON GODDESS sitting at mid center.)

GRIOT: The lake was boundless, and the roof above shone with millions of precious gems! In the center of the lake was an island, where a beautiful Moon Goddess sat on an emerald throne. As Zandilli stared in wonder, a flotilla of tiny Water Lillies swam to him and brought him across the lake to the island.

(Offstage chorus sings. MUSIC: "Sapphire Lake." Water Lillies dance to Zandilli, take him to Moon Goddess; Zandilli kneels before her as Water Lillies stand behind throne.)

MOON GODDESS: Welcome to the land of the Moon People, Zandilli! We have been expecting you!

ZANDILLI: O great Goddess! I have come in search of my lost spear! I have only three more days to find it, or the Princess will be wed to another!

MOON GODDESS: The spear is within your reach. It fell at the mouth of the cave and was placed in our treasure trove. To take it back you must perform two tasks, which will prove your worthiness to wed the Princess. If you fail in these tasks, you will die!

ZANDILLI: I accept the challenge, O Goddess! Show me the first task!

MOON GODDESS: In the far corner of the cave, there is a black chamber — a room so filled with darkness that it resists all light. You must make this chamber as bright and beautiful as our other rooms.

(LIGHTS FADE OUT EXCEPT FOR SPOTLIGHT ON ZANDILLI, who crosses to down center.)

GRIOT: Zandilli was taken to the black chamber. He was greatly saddened.

ZANDILLI: If only the Moon Goddess had given me a task of strength and courage! That I could perform! But to make a room like this bright and beautiful? I must prepare to die! *(sits down, facing audience)*

GRIOT: But as Zandilli sat in the black chamber, he began to think of all the wonderful things of the world he would never see again. He would never see the Princess. He would never see flowers. He would never see the birds nor the butterflies—

ZANDILLI: Butterflies! Of course! Butterflies! *(stands)* "Butterfly, butterfly, fluttering free; send your comfort quick to me."

(LIGHTS FLICKER.)

BUTTERFLY: *(o.s.)* I hear your cry, Zandilli. And I shall send you assistance right away!

(LIGHTS FADE UP as THREE FIREFLIES dance out from left, waving glittering, brightly-colored cloths as they surround Zandilli for a few seconds then exit left. MUSIC: "Dance of the Fireflies.")

GRIOT: Within an instant, a swarm of butterflies and fireflies flew into the room! They spread themselves across the walls of the black chamber and made it sparkle with light and beauty!

(Zandilli dashes up to Moon Goddess.)

ZANDILLI: O Goddess, I have completed the first task!

MOON GODDESS: Congratulations, Zandilli, your spear is partly won. Here is your second task. *(motions to Water Lillies)* Do you see the shining robes of my attendants? They are made from the gossamer wings of water flies. You must fill a hundred of our boats with water fly wings by this time tomorrow — or you will die!

(LIGHTS FADE OUT EXCEPT FOR SPOTLIGHT ON ZANDILLI, who crosses to down center.)

GRIOT: Zandilli was taken to the storehouse, where he sat among a hundred empty boats. Again, he was greatly saddened.

ZANDILLI: Fill a hundred boats with water fly wings? This task is even more hopeless than the first! I must prepare to die! *(sits down, facing audience)*

GRIOT: And so Zandilli sat, utterly discouraged, thinking of all the wonderful things of the world he would never see again.

ZANDILLI: I will never see the Princess. I will never see my parents. I will never see the cool mountain stream where I saved Frog from Vulture. I will — wait a moment! Of course! The Frog! *(stands)* "Frog of the forest, Frog of the wood; aid me in my quest for good."

(LIGHTS FLICKER.)

FROG: *(o.s.)* I hear your cry, Zandilli. And I shall come to your aid immediately!

(LIGHTS FADE UP as THREE LIZARDS dance out from left, each carrying a stack of water fly wings; they dance by Zandilli, then dance to mid center where they deposit stacks at feet of Moon Goddess and exit left. MUSIC: "Dance of the Fireflies.")

GRIOT: Within an instant, an army of frogs and lizards appeared, catching thousands of flies until each one of the hundred boats was filled with water fly wings!
(Zandilli dashes up to Moon Goddess.)

ZANDILLI: O Goddess, the second task is complete! May I have the lost spear?

MOON GODDESS: Zandilli, you are the most marvelous mortal that has ever existed! The griots will sing of your adventures till the end of time!

(Water Lilly #1 hands spear to Moon Goddess, who presents it to Zandilli.)

MOON GODDESS: Here is your spear! Hurry back to your homeland, for the Princess is going to be wed when the sun rises tomorrow!

(LIGHTS FADE DOWN on Moon Goddess and Water Lillies; SPOTLIGHT follows Zandilli as he crosses to down left where King stands between Princess and Suitor #1 as Suitors #2 and 3 look on; LIGHTS UP FULL.)

SUITOR #2: Look! Zandilli has returned!

SUITOR #3: And he is carrying the lost spear!

PRINCESS: *(runs to Zandilli)* I will marry Zandilli!

KING: The gods have spoken! Destiny has decreed this marriage! Let the wedding proceed!

SUITORS #1, 2 & 3: Zandilli! Zandilli! Zandilli!

(MUSIC: instrumental introduction to "Sapphire Lake"; Entire Cast dances onstage and gathers around Zandilli and Princess at down center.)

GRIOT: And that, People of the Kingdom, is the tale of Zandilli and The Lost Spear. Always remember — it was not only Zandilli's strength and courage that won him the Princess...it was the kindness he showed to others. *(Entire Cast sings. MUSIC: "Sapphire Lake.")*

(LIGHTS OUT.)

THE END

Zandilli's Walking Song
(by L.E. McCullough)

♩ = 150

La- la- la- la- la la- la- la- la La- la- la- la- la

la- la- la- la La- la- la- la- la la- la- la- la

La- la- la- la- la la- la- la- la

Sapphire Lake
(by L.E. McCullough)

Sapphire Lake, pg. 2

Dance of the Fireflies
(by L.E. McCullough)

Dance of the Fireflies, pg. 2

la- la- la- la- la- la- la- la- la- la- la- la- la-

la- la- la- la- la- la- la-

la- la- la- la

la- la- la- la

© L.E. McCullough 1997

Call of the Griot

(by L.E. McCullough)

The Magic Ring

This tale from Italy is believed to have originated in Central Asia, possibly migrating westward to Europe with Marco Polo's return from China in the 13th century. In many fairy tales, a luckless or witless human is rescued by more competent and clear-thinking animal chums — the French tale *Puss in Boots* is a well-known example. Of course, the naive Gigi should have been doubly-warned of his beloved's impending treachery…"Maliarda" is Italian for "enchantress" or "witch."

RUNNING TIME: 20 minutes

PLACE: Italy

CAST: 13 actors, min. 4 boys, 5 girls

Gigi	Gigi's Mother
Dog	Old Woman
Cat	Waiter
Maliarda	3 Servants
Maliarda's Mother	Maliarda's Father
Mouse	

STAGE SET: stool at down right; stool at down left

PROPS: large jar, ring, push cart, bowl, mirror, cloak, swivel chair, 2 pillow cushions, bowl

COSTUMES: Humans wear medieval garb appropriate to their occupation and station; Animals wear appropriate masks and body coverings

(LIGHTS UP FULL on GIGI, standing, and GIGI'S MOTHER sitting on stool at down right.)

GIGI'S MOTHER: *(to audience)* Buon giorno! This is my only son, Gigi. Say hello to the nice people, Gigi.

GIGI: Hello to the nice people, Gigi!

GIGI'S MOTHER: Every mother should have a son as good as my Gigi. But, like most sons, the day came at last when he decided he had to go out into the world and bring back his fortune.

GIGI: Mother, the day has come at last when I have decided I must go out into the world and bring back my fortune.

GIGI'S MOTHER: *(sighs)* It must be Tuesday already! Then be careful, Gigi.

GIGI: I will, mother.

(Gigi starts to walk left but stops, when his mother speaks.)

GIGI'S MOTHER: And always be kind to whomever you meet!

GIGI: I will, mother.

GIGI'S MOTHER: And remember to help others in need!

GIGI: I will, mother.

GIGI'S MOTHER: And look both ways before you cross a busy street!

GIGI: I will, mother.

GIGI'S MOTHER: And brush your teeth between meals and after snacks.

GIGI: I will, mother.

GIGI'S MOTHER: And don't forget—

GIGI: I will, mother. I will-I will-I will-I will! Ciao!

GIGI'S MOTHER: Arrivederci, mio bambino!

(OLD WOMAN hobbles onstage from left, toting a large jar on her shoulder.)

GIGI: I believe the first town is a few miles ahead. And look, there is an old woman! See how she struggles with that jar! Saluto, signora! May I assist you?

OLD WOMAN: *(puts down jar)* Yes, young man. I live just around the bend. Follow me.

(Gigi picks up jar and follows Old Woman who hobbles to down left; Gigi puts jar down next to stool.)

OLD WOMAN: Sit down and rest yourself. My house is poor, but you are welcome.

GIGI: I have a very long way before me, signora, but a seat in your chimney corner I will not refuse.

OLD WOMAN: And where are you going, young man?

GIGI: Out into the world to bring back my fortune!

OLD WOMAN: The world is very big and full of wonders. But it can also be very lonely. Perhaps you should have company when you travel?

GIGI: But I have no friends, signora.

OLD WOMAN: What about your mother? Is she not your friend?

GIGI: Of course. But she must stay at home and worry about me.

OLD WOMAN: Then you may take my dog and cat. Here, Cané! Here, Gatto!

(DOG and CAT enter on all fours from left.)

DOG: Woof!

CAT: Maiow!

GIGI: These will be excellent company!

OLD WOMAN: They are wiser than most of their kind. But now you have three mouths to feed instead of just one. Here, I have something that may help you in time of need.

(She takes a ring from her pocket and gives it to Gigi.)

GIGI: This is a very beautiful ring!

OLD WOMAN: It is a magic ring. When you want anything very much, just give it a twist on your finger. Then you will see what you will see! But never, *never* lose it or give it away. *(exits right)*

GIGI: Grazie, signora! Come, amici! Let us see the world!

(Gigi puts ring in his pocket and walks upstage, going around the stage counterclockwise, followed by Dog and Cat.)

GIGI'S MOTHER: Normally, I would be very concerned about my only son speaking to strangers. But this was quite an adventure for Gigi! He and his new friends, the dog and cat, walked for many miles until they found themselves in a forest.

(Gigi, Dog and Cat stop at down center.)

GIGI: My friends, it is getting dark. The woods give us shelter, but there is nothing to eat.

DOG: Perhaps you should take out the magic ring the Old Woman gave you and wish for food.

GIGI: Yes, that would be— *(double takes)* A talking dog! I cannot believe my ears!

CAT: Then believe your stomach. Cané is right, amico; give the magic ring a twist so we can have supper.

GIGI: But of course, I should have known! A magic ring and talking animals! This is a wonderful adventure!

DOG: The ring, if you please.

GIGI: Certainly. *(takes out ring, puts it on finger, gives it a twist)* I wish a table could be set before me now. A table with a fine, tasty supper upon it.

CAT: Ahem.

GIGI: Oh, yes, with a delicate morsel of fish for Gatto—
DOG: Woof!
GIGI: And a juicy bone for Cané.
CAT: Grazie!

(WAITER enters from left pushing a food cart to down center; Gigi takes a bowl of food from cart; Gigi, Dog and Cat mime eating.)

WAITER: Buon appetito! *(stands behind cart)*
GIGI: An entire feast in the middle of nowhere! I cannot believe this is happening!
CAT: Wait until you see the bill.
DOG: This is the most delicious meal I have ever eaten! Woof!

(Gigi hands bowl to Waiter, who bows, puts bowl on cart and exits with cart offstage right.)

GIGI: I wonder what I should wish for next? I can think of hundreds of things — gold and silver, fine clothes, a big house, some horses, maybe a big battleship to sail in the ocean!
CAT: I would settle for a few acres of fresh catnip.
DOG: Put me down for an endless supply of soup bones.
GIGI: Ah! But how silly I am! My mother always said that people lose their heads when good luck comes their way. I think I will keep mine on my shoulders. Let us save our wishes until we see something we really want, eh, my friends?
DOG: Woof!
CAT: Maiow!

(Gigi, Dog and Cat lay down to sleep.)

GIGI'S MOTHER: That's my Gigi. Very prudent. Very careful. And always thinking of his mother. Battleship, indeed! The next morning, Gigi and his friends rose up early and set off down the road.

(Gigi, Dog and Cat awake and rise; they march in place at down center.)

GIGI: There is nothing so fine in all the world as waking up to a beautiful morning! Do I wish for a stately horse and carriage? Not when I have two good legs to carry me along!

DOG: What do you wish for, then? Do you wish for great wisdom and knowledge?

GIGI: What use have I for them? I am not a scholar!

CAT: Do you wish for great strength and power?

GIGI: What use have I for them? I am not a warrior!

DOG: Do you wish for great wealth and riches?

GIGI: What use have I for them? I am not an aristocrat!

CAT: Do you wish for the hand and heart of that beautiful maiden looking out the window?

GIGI: What use have I for them? I am not — *(double takes)* What maiden, where?

(MALIARDA enters from left and stands at down left, checking her reflection in a mirror; Gigi nearly swoons but is steadied by Dog and Cat.)

GIGI: That is the most beautiful girl in all the world!

DOG: Just as I suspected — he is crazy for love!

CAT: The worst kind of desire!

GIGI: I must speak to her at once and tell her of my affection! But, no — I am just a poor peasant boy! She would never speak to me! Look at her splendid mansion! Look at her gorgeous clothes!

DOG: Look at the magic ring on your finger.

GIGI: Eh? Oh, yes, the ring...do you suppose it is possible?

CAT: If it can get room service in the middle of a forest, it can probably whip up some new clothes and a hair makeover.

GIGI: *(holds out finger, twists ring)* I wish for a mansion to be built right here. A mansion filled with fine furniture and priceless art.

DOG: Woof!

GIGI: And clothes! I need new clothes, plenty of food and drink and servants.

CAT: Maiow!

GIGI: Oh, yes, and nice soft pillows for my friends!

(THREE SERVANTS enter from left; SERVANT #1 carries a fancy cloak he puts around Gigi, SERVANT #2 rolls in a swivel chair he has Gigi sit in, SERVANT #3 carries two pillow cushions he puts down next to Dog and Cat. Servants stand behind Gigi, Dog and Cat.)

GIGI: This is most incredible! We are sitting in the middle of a palace — where moments ago there was nothing but a field!

DOG: And here come the neighbors.

(As Servants exit right, MALIARDA'S MOTHER and MALIARDA'S FATHER enter from left; they take Maliarda by the arms and present her to Gigi.)

MALIARDA'S FATHER: *(bows)* Signore! We are pleased to have such an eminent gentleman living next to us!

GIGI: *(to Dog and Cat)* Did you hear that? He called me "a gentleman"!

CAT: What he doesn't know won't hurt us.

MALIARDA'S MOTHER: Perhaps you would care to make the acquaintance of our only daughter, Maliarda?

GIGI: *(to Dog and Cat)* Would a pig care to make the acquaintance of mud?

(Maliarda steps forward, curtseys and beams at Gigi, who beams back at her as Maliarda's Mother and Father step to down left and converse secretively.)

MALIARDA'S MOTHER: This silly boy must be a prince!

MALIARDA'S FATHER: Or some sort of wizard!

MALIARDA'S MOTHER: We must have our daughter marry him!

MALIARDA'S FATHER: And then we can partake of his boundless wealth!

MALIARDA: Mother! Father! Gigi has asked me to marry him!

DOG: That was awfully quick!

MALIARDA'S MOTHER: Come, we must prepare for the wedding! *(exits left with Maliarda)*

MALIARDA'S FATHER: *(shakes Gigi's hand)* Glad to have you in the family — son! *(exits left)*

GIGI: Did you hear that? He called me "son"!

CAT: I'm calling you an idiot! Those people only want your money!

GIGI: That is not so! Maliarda cares about me for myself!

DOG: Right — like a hungry fox cares about a chicken!

CAT: No use trying to reason with him! He's caught a bad case of puppy love!

DOG: Please!

GIGI: In fact, I told her that a few days ago I was just a poor peasant boy.

CAT: Uh-oh...

GIGI: And that all my wealth and fine furnishings came from this magic ring. I had to be truthful!

DOG: The truth hurts...

CAT: This truth is *really* going to hurt!

GIGI: And even with that, she said she still wanted to marry me! *(sighs)* My beautiful, beautiful, Maliarda!

(Waiter enters from right carrying a bowl he hands to Gigi.)

GIGI: Ah, it is time for supper! Let us eat and be merry, my friends, for tomorrow I wed the love of my life!

(Gigi sips from bowl, hands it back to Waiter, who exits right.)

GIGI: That was delicious! *(yawns)* My, but I am sleepy! Sooooo sleeeeepy...

(Dog and Cat yawn, lay down on pillows and sleep; Gigi slumps in chair and nods asleep. Maliarda enters from left and crosses stealthily to Gigi as Maliarda's Mother and Father stand at down left.)

MALIARDA'S MOTHER: You put the sleeping potion in Gigi's supper?

MALIARDA'S FATHER: And in the water of the Dog and Cat as well. They will be quite surprised when they awake!

(Maliarda takes the ring from his finger and faces audience; she puts the ring on her finger and gives it a twist.)

MALIARDA: I wish that Gigi's palace be moved to the highest, steepest, snowiest, farthest peak of yonder mountain range!

(LIGHTS OUT BRIEFLY as Maliarda and her parents exit left and chair, cloak and pillows are removed; SPOTLIGHT DOWN CENTER on Gigi, Dog and Cat awaking.)

GIGI: *(shivers)* Brrrr, it is very cold! Why, someone has left the window open! *(stands, looks out at audience)* Wait a minute! What are these mountains doing outside my palace window? And where did all this snow come from?

DOG: And where is your magic ring?

GIGI: And where is Maliarda's house?

CAT: And where is your magic ring?

GIGI: And where are my servants?

DOG: And where is your magic ring?

GIGI: And where is my magic ring? *(double takes, holds up finger)* My magic ring! It is gone!

CAT: Maiow!

DOG: Woof!

CAT: Those are animal words for "it is up to us to save this poor lad from himself"!

GIGI: My friends, it appears we have been bewitched! Who could have done such a thing?

DOG: I suppose we better spell it out for him.

CAT: M-A...

DOG: L-I...

CAT: A-R...

DOG: D-A.

CAT: With an emphasis on L-I-A-R.

GIGI: Maliarda! Do you think she has been bewitched as well?

DOG: We think Maliarda has done the bewitching!

GIGI: But of course! I told her about the ring! She has deceived me! Aaugh! Now I see everything so clearly!

CAT: Do you also see a way to get down from this mountain?

GIGI: I do not! Unless you, my loyal four-footed friends, can climb down this treacherous, icy slope, retrieve the magic ring from Maliarda and bring it back to me!

DOG: I suppose we could do that. What do you think, Gatto?

CAT: I think if we make it to flat ground, we head for the beach and lose the peasant boy.

DOG: Woof!

CAT: Maiow!

DOG: Grrrr!

CAT: Hssss!

DOG: Grrrrrrrrwoof!

CAT: Hsssssssrrow!

DOG: Grrrrrrwoof!

CAT: All right, have it your way. We get the ring and bring it back. *(to Gigi)* It is going to cost you plenty of catnip!

GIGI: Thank you, my friends! Farewell and good hunting!

(LIGHTS OUT as Gigi exits left.)

GIGI'S MOTHER: I am so glad I did not know what danger had befallen my Gigi. A mother always worries about her child — especially when his life depends upon the cleverness of a dog and a cat! But these two animals lost no time in getting down the mountain. At the hour of midnight, they silently entered Maliarda's house.

(LIGHTS UP FULL; Dog and Cat crouch at down center.)

DOG: This is a pretty nice house.

CAT: Of course it is! They got it by wishing on Gigi's magic ring!

DOG: *(points left)* Is that Maliarda's room?

CAT: Yes, and the door is shut.

DOG: How are we going to get inside?

CAT: Let me think. Ssshhh!

(MOUSE scurries onstage from right; Cat stalks her.)

DOG: It is a mouse!

CAT: I know that!

DOG: Say, this is no time to play a cat-and-mouse game!

CAT: This is no game!

(Cat springs and catches Mouse, who lies on her back in terror.)

MOUSE: Eeek! Eeek! Please do not kill me, Signor Gatto!

CAT: Oooh, what a tasty mouthful you would make! But I have other business with you, Signora Topa. How would you like to do a small errand for me?

MOUSE: Yes, yes, anything you say! Just spare my life!

CAT: I will spare your life, if — and only if — you succeed in gnawing a hole through this door.

MOUSE: I can do that! Mice have sharp teeth!

CAT: (*bares teeth to Mouse*) So do cats! Come on, get to work!

(*Mouse goes to down left and mimes gnawing on door, as Cat crouches behind her.*)

DOG: Gatto, you are mad! It will take that mouse all night to gnaw a hole big enough for you to get through.

CAT: But *I* am not going through. Say, cheese-breath, are you finished?

MOUSE: Not quite. I have made only a small hole, just big enough for a tiny mouse like myself.

(*Cat slaps paw on Mouse's shoulder.*)

MOUSE: Eeek! I think I have said something very bad.

CAT: Now, if you *really* want me to spare your life, you will slip through that hole—

MOUSE: Eeek!

CAT: Jump on the lady's bed—

MOUSE: Eeek!

CAT: Bite her finger very softly—

MOUSE: Eeek!

CAT: So she takes off the ring—

MOUSE: Eeek! Eeek!

CAT: Without waking—

MOUSE: Eeek! Eeek! Eeek!

CAT: I said, *without* waking—

(*Mouse silently mouths "Eeek!"*)

CAT: And then bring the ring to me. Capiche?

(Mouse nods "yes" vigorously.)

CAT: Andate! Go!

(Mouse scurries offstage left.)

DOG: You are the clever one!
CAT: And I have six lives yet to go!
DOG: A-ha! Our associate returns!

(Mouse scurries onstage from left.)

MOUSE: A small problem, signori. The lady has no ring on her finger.
CAT: No ring? *(pounces on Mouse)* Tell the truth or die!
MOUSE: Eeek! I am telling the truth! The lady has no ring on her finger!
DOG: Wait! It must then be in her mouth. Go back and swish her nose with your tail. She will open her mouth to sneeze, and the ring will drop out.

(Cat releases Mouse, who scurries offstage left.)

CAT: *(to Dog)* Her mouth?
DOG: Really quite logical. You see, the superior breed of animal maintains the habit of active chewing—
CAT: Save it for your memoirs. Here comes Mouse with the ring.

(Mouse scurries onstage from left and presents ring to Cat.)

MOUSE: There you go, gentlemen. *(begins backing offstage right)* If you don't mind, I'll just be on my way—

CAT: Not so fast!

(*Mouse freezes in terror, mouths "Eeek!"*)

DOG: Thank you, Mouse. Our master owes his life to you.

(*Mouse exhales in relief.*)

CAT: Now, get out of here! Andate!

(*Mouse scurries offstage right.*)

MOUSE: Eeek! Eeek! Eeek! Eeek!
DOG: We must get back to Gigi!
CAT: Maiow!
DOG: Woof!

(*Dog and Cat exit left; Gigi's Mother crosses to down center and addresses audience.*)

GIGI'S MOTHER: After Gigi got back the magic ring, he wished himself and the Dog and Cat away from the mountain.
GIGI: (*o.s.*) Huzzah! We are free!
GIGI'S MOTHER: And he wished Maliarda and her evil parents *up* on the mountain!
MALIARDA, MALIARDA'S MOTHER & FATHER: (*o.s.*) Aiiiieeee!
GIGI'S MOTHER: But only for a day or two, because my Gigi is not a vengeful boy, even to those who have done him wrong. Oh, how happy I was to see him when he returned home!

(*Gigi enters from left and crosses to down center, followed by Dog and Cat.*)

GIGI: *(hugs Mother)* Hello, mother! It is wonderful to see you again!

GIGI'S MOTHER: How I have missed you, my son! Did you find your fortune?

GIGI: *(holds up hand with ring)* It is here in my hand!

GIGI'S MOTHER: *(grabs his hand)* A tattoo on your thumb? Oh, Gigi, how could you?

GIGI: No, this ring on my finger! It is a magic ring! I can wish for anything, and it comes true!

GIGI'S MOTHER: Then please wish for that tattoo to go away!

GIGI: All right, but first, let us eat! *(snaps fingers)* Waiter! Bring in the banquet!

(Waiter enters from right pushing food cart, followed by Three Servants who bring out swivel chair, cloak and pillows as before; they put cloak on Mother and sit her in chair with pillows, then stand with Waiter behind.)

GIGI'S MOTHER: Gigi, that ring has the power to bring evil into your life as well as good.

GIGI: I know, mother. Without the loyalty of this dog and cat I would have frozen to death on the mountain. The power of their friendship is far greater than the power of this ring.

DOG: He is a good boy, our master!

CAT: Sure, but can't he use that ring to whip up a nice bucket of sardines?

GIGI: *(takes off ring and gives to Mother)* Keep this ring for me, mother. The Old Woman said to use it when I wanted something very much. With my family and my friends here, I have truly found my fortune.

(LIGHTS OUT.)

THE END

The Six Swans

This German tale appeared in the first edition of fairy tales published in 1812 by The Brothers Grimm titled *Children's and Household Tales*, a marvelous collection of folklore known today the world over as "Grimm's Fairy Tales." Jakob Ludwig Karl Grimm (1785–1863) and Wilhelm Karl Grimm (1786–1859) were trained as linguists, and their early interest in ancient languages led to their lifelong work of collecting folk stories and fairy tales. *The Six Swans* was obtained from a family friend, Dortchen Wild (1795–1867), who married Wilhelm in 1825.

RUNNING TIME: 15 minutes

PLACE: Germany

CAST: 15 actors, min. 8 boys, 3 girls

Narrator	King
Witch	Witch's Daughter/Queen
6 King's Sons	Lili, King's Daughter
Prince	3 Servants

STAGE SET: large boulder at mid center; bench at down left

PROPS: bow, 2 white towels, torch, cloak, tiara, bracelet

COSTUMES: Characters wear medieval garb appropriate to their occupation and station; King's sons wear swan heads and wings when appearing as swans

(LIGHTS UP FULL on NARRATOR standing at down right; KING enters from left, carrying a bow; King dashes about excitedly, then slows down and stands at down center.)

NARRATOR: *(to audience)* Once upon a time, a very long time ago, there lived a King. One day the King went hunting in the great Black Forest. In his eagerness pursuing the prey, he became separated from his party. By nightfall, he was completely lost.

KING: *(calls out)* Hallooo! Hallooo! Is anyone near? Can anyone hear me?

WITCH: *(o.s. left)* I hear you!

KING: Thank goodness! Someone is at hand!

(King walks to stage left as WITCH enters from stage left, hobbling slowly.)

KING: Good madame, can you show me out of this forest? I am the King, and I must get back to my court!

WITCH: I know well who you are, my lord. And I can show you out of the forest. But on one condition.

KING: One condition? You demand a condition of the King?

WITCH: I do. I have a daughter. She is as beautiful as any girl in the world. If you promise to make her your Queen, I will show you safely out of the forest.

(WITCH'S DAUGHTER enters from left and curtseys before the King.)

WITCH: Here she comes now. Is she not a most desirable girl?

NARRATOR: Now the King's first Queen had died some years before. Even so, he did not wish to marry at this time. And though the Witch's Daughter was very pretty, there was something about her that made the King shudder with fear.

KING: She is...pleasing...to look upon.

WITCH: Marry her, then, and you shall return safely to your court.

NARRATOR: The King had no choice. So he agreed to the bargain and made the Witch's Daughter his new Queen.

(*King takes hand of Witch's Daughter and strides off-stage left, followed by Witch, who hobbles behind them, cackling. KING'S SIX SONS enter from right, followed by LILI, KING'S DAUGHTER; they gather in a line at down center facing audience.*)

NARRATOR: From his first marriage, the King had six sons and one daughter. He loved these children more than anything in the world, and he was greatly afraid his new Queen might try to harm them. So he hid them in a lonely castle on a high mountain. When he thought the Queen would not notice, he would visit them.

(*Six Sons and Lili scurry behind large boulder at mid center; Witch's Daughter/Queen enters from left carrying a white towel; she crosses stealthily to the boulder.*)

NARRATOR: But the Queen *did* notice and soon discovered the castle where the King's children were hidden. One day, the Queen made several white shirts that each contained a charm. She took these into the forest with her. When she got close to the castle, the King's Sons, thinking it was their father the King who had come to see them, rushed outside.

(*Six Sons rush out from behind boulder; Queen strikes each with the towel, and each Son screams and dashes offstage left followed by laughing Queen.*)

NARRATOR: But the evil Queen threw one of the enchanted shirts over each Son, changing him instantly into a swan! As the Queen laughed with merriment, the swans took flight and soared away out of the forest. The Queen thought she had gotten rid of the King's children forever!

(Lili emerges cautiously from behind boulder.)

NARRATOR: But the Queen did not know of the King's Daughter, whose name was Lili. This young girl had not run out with her brothers, and she had seen the terrible thing the Queen had done.

LILI: My brothers have flown far away. I must leave this place and find them.

(Lili walks around stage, coming back to boulder.)

NARRATOR: Lili searched for many days. Finally, after crossing into another country, she saw a small hut.

LILI: There is a room with six beds! And in the kitchen, I see six chairs, with six sets of plates around the table!

(Lili sits in front of boulder, curled up as if asleep.)

NARRATOR: Lili hid underneath one of the beds and waited. Near nightfall, there came a noise of great rustling wings. Six white swans appeared, but Lili knew the swans were her brothers.

(Six Sons, wearing swan heads and wings, twirl onstage from left; they stop at boulder and take off swan heads.)

LILI: *(rises)* My brothers! You are alive!
SON #1: It is our sister, Lili!
SON #2: We can stay with you but a quarter hour!

SON #3: For that length of time we become human once again!

SON #4: After that, we are changed back into swans!

LILI: Can nothing be done to free you from this terrible spell?

SON #5: There is, dear sister. But it is too hard. We cannot ask it of you.

SON #6: For six whole years you would have to remain silent —

SON #1: Never to speak or laugh —

SON #2: And during that six years you would have to make six shirts for us—

SON #3: Each made from fresh aster down that you have gathered by night —

SON #4: If you fail in any of these things, dear sister —

SON #5: We would be lost to the spell forever!

SON #6: Brothers! The time is past! We are losing our humanity!

(Sons put on swan heads and twirl offstage left.)

LILI: No sacrifice is too great to save my brothers! I will begin gathering the aster down at once!

(Lili mimes picking aster down from ground and putting it in her pockets; PRINCE enters from left and sees her.)

NARRATOR: Lili spent many nights gathering aster down and many days spinning the down into flax. One day, the Prince of the country was walking through the forest and saw her.

PRINCE: Hello, fair maiden!

(Lili is startled and backs a step away.)

PRINCE: There is no need to be afraid. I am the Prince of this country, and I mean you no harm. *(pause)* Still no reply? You poor, sorrowful maiden. Perhaps the power of speech has been taken from you by some wicked fiend? I shall avenge you! Come to my palace, and I will give you the freedom of my household.

(Prince leads Lili to down left; THREE SERVANTS enter from left and put on her a cloak, a tiara and bracelet.)

NARRATOR: At the Prince's castle, Lili was dressed in the most glorious of rich garments, but not a single word would she speak. Her modesty and gentleness so pleased the Prince, that he chose her for his wife, and they were married. Yet even so, Lili spoke not a word but continued for several years to weave and sew the shirts for her brothers.

(Prince and Lili sit on bench; Witch hobbles onstage from left.)

NARRATOR: There was one old woman in the palace who began to spread ugly rumours about the Prince's new wife.

WITCH: *(to Servants)* The poor dumb thing! Who knows where this pitiful maid came from!

SERVANT #1: Perhaps she is a beggar!

SERVANT #2: Or a thief come to steal the Prince's fortune!

WITCH: Or even a witch who has cast a spell upon his heart!

PRINCE: *(stands)* I will hear no gossip about my wife!

SERVANT #3: Then why doesn't she tell us herself?

PRINCE: *(to Lili)* Darling, can you speak?

(Lili nods her head "yes.")

PRINCE: Will you speak?

(Lili nods her head "no.")

WITCH: There, you see! She hides a false heart!

SERVANT #1: And what is it she is always sewing so secretly?

SERVANT #2: Show us!

SERVANT #3: Tell us!

SERVANTS #1, 2 & 3: Show us! Tell us! Show us! Tell us!
Show us! Tell us!

(Lili hides her head in her hands.)

PRINCE: Enough!

WITCH: The law demands that one accused as a witch sub-
mit to trial by fire!

SERVANTS #1, 2 & 3: Burn her at the stake! Burn her at the
stake!

*(Servants #1, 2 & 3 take Lili to mid center and put her
up against boulder; Prince and Witch follow and stand
to right of boulder; King and Queen enter from left and
watch from mid left.)*

NARRATOR: On the day of Lili's trial, a huge crowd from
across Europe gathered in front of the palace. Even her
father, the King, and his new Queen were among the
onlookers. But though her life was in danger, Lili would
not say a word to save herself.

PRINCE: My darling, please! Please say just one word in your
defense!

*(Lili does not reply, but turns her head away from
Prince.)*

SERVANT #1: Executioner! Light the fire!

*(Servant #3 approaches Lili with a torch; a rustling
noise comes from offstage left.)*

NARRATOR: Just as the fire was about to be lit, a most extra-ordinary thing took place!

(Six Sons wearing swan outfits twirl onstage from left and "fly" around the stage.)

SERVANT #2: Six white swans! See how they circle the Princess!

SERVANT #3: Look, she is throwing something upon them!

(Lili pulls a white towel from her pocket and strikes each Brother with the towel as they pass her, where-upon they shed their swan costumes and embrace Lili.)

NARRATOR: It was the very last day of the six years during which Lili had neither spoken nor laughed. And the night before, she had finished the very last shirt. As Lili touched each swan with a shirt —

SERVANT #1: The swans! They are changing!

SERVANT #2: They have become men!

KING: My sons! And my daughter, Lili!

LILI: My Prince, at last I may dare speak! These are my brothers, who were made into swans by that hideous woman! *(points at Queen)*

PRINCE: Seize her at once!

(Servants #2 & 3 seize Queen.)

KING: *(points to Witch, who has tried to sneak offstage right)* And there is the mother witch who forced me to marry her evil daughter!

(Servant #1 seizes Witch.)

PRINCE: *(to Lili)* It is clear now why you have not spoken all these years. Your silence was necessary for you to break your brothers' spell.

LILI: Are you angry I did not confide in you, my husband?

PRINCE: Angry? By no means! You have proven to be loyal and trustworthy — qualities any Prince should prize in a Princess! Come, let us rule wisely and in harmony!

(LIGHTS OUT.)

THE END

Squeak and Maiow!

These three tales from Wales (*The Cat and the Mouse*), the Congo (*The Cat and the Rat*) and ancient Greece (*The Lion and the Mouse*) explore the longstanding relationship — usually antagonistic — between the feline and rodent families. Fairy tales contain much folklore about cats, mainly concerning how they can predict changes in weather or the coming of company and good and bad luck. The mouse and rat are almost always portrayed as bad, mischievous creatures, sometimes even the representatives or personification of the Devil. However, they are sometimes seen as helpful animals, as in Aesop's *The Lion and the Mouse*. Aesop is believed to have been born about 620 B.C. on the Greek island of Samos and to have lived until 564 B.C. He took tales current among the Greeks of his time as well as older stories from India and the Middle East, using animals to cleverly depict the follies and foibles of humans. The first collection of *Aesop's Fables* was published around 300 B.C.; the first edition to include all 231 known Aesop's Fables was published in Germany in 1810.

RUNNING TIME: 15 minutes

PLACE: The Animal Kingdom

CAST: 10 actors plus chorus, min. 6 boys, 2 girls

Cat	Miss Mouse
Miss Cow	Farmer
Butcher	Baker
Rat	Lion
2 Hunters	Offstage Chorus

STAGE SET: stool at down right

PROPS: pitchfork, drumstick, bread loaf, handful of hay, milk carton with straw, kazoo, net

MUSIC: *The Mousie Leapt*; *Old MacDonald Had a Farm*; *We Can Make Our Friendship Strong*

COSTUMES: Animals wear appropriate masks and body coverings; Farmer can wear overalls; Butcher a white apron and Baker a chef's hat; Rat wears sunglasses, tropical shirt and hat; Hunters wear camouflage outfits

---

(LIGHTS UP FULL on CAT perched, apparently asleep, on stool at down right. MOUSE creeps slowly onstage from left, "Ssshhing!" the audience; when Mouse reaches down center, Cat awakes, hisses loudly and leaps off the stool to chase the giggling, squeaking Mouse offstage right.)

CAT: I'll get you next time, you miserable rodent! *(to audience)* Oh, hello! I'm Cat. That was Mouse. We have a what you'd call "a relationship"... a mutual history that goes back a looooong ways. Basically, it works like this — Mouse tries to grab bits of food for her dinner. I try to grab bits of Mouse for *my* dinner. Here are some stories about how it all started. Like this one from England.

(Mouse enters from left, whistling; as Mouse passes, Cat bites Mouse's tail off and runs with it to down right, jumping back up on stool and waving the tail in its paws.)

MOUSE: Owwww! That hurt! *(to audience)* Did you see that? That cat bit my tail off! *(crosses to down right)* Pray, Cat, give me back my tail!

CAT: No can do. I'll not give you back your tail, till you go to the cow and fetch me some milk. Mmmm… delicious, yummy-yummy milk…

MOUSE: Well, if you're going to be that way about it!

(COW enters from right and meanders to down center.)

MOUSE: Oh, there is a cow!

(Mouse crosses to Cow as CHORUS sings offstage. MUSIC: "The Mousie Leapt.")

CHORUS: *(sings)*
The Mousie leapt, and skittered away,
Till she came to the Cow and thus did say:

MOUSE: Dear Miss Cow, pray give me milk, that I may give Cat milk, that Cat may give me my tail back again!

COW: Hmmm. Sounds reasonable. But I won't give you any milk until you go to the Farmer and get me some hay.

MOUSE: It's a deal! Just stay there and graze while I go get the Farmer.

(Cow moves to mid center as FARMER enters from left carrying a pitchfork and making hay-baling motions at down left.)

MOUSE: There he is! *(waves)* Farmer, oh Farmer!

CHORUS: *(sings)*
The Mousie leapt, and skittered away,
Till she came to the Farmer and thus did say:

MOUSE: Dear Farmer, pray give me hay, that I may give Cow hay, that Cow may give me milk, that I may give Cat milk, that Cat may give me my tail back again!

FARMER: Well, I reckon I have some hay to spare. But I'm mighty hungry. If you go to the Butcher and get me some meat, I'll give you some hay.

MOUSE: Consider it done! Oh, where oh where oh where can I find a Butcher? (crosses right)

FARMER: (resumes hay-baling while moving to mid center) A nice juicy steak would suit me fine!

(BUTCHER enters from right carrying a drumstick.)

MOUSE: Ah! There's a friendly Butcher!

CHORUS: (sings)
The Mousie leapt, and skittered away,
Till she came to the Butcher and thus did say:

MOUSE: Dear Butcher, I have a small request. Can you give me some meat, so that I may give Farmer meat, that Farmer may give me hay, that I may give Cow hay, that Cow may give me milk, that I may give Cat milk, that Cat may give me my tail back again?

BUTCHER: So you want *me* to give *you* meat?

MOUSE: I believe that's what I said, yes. Wasn't it?

BUTCHER: Hmmm. I suppose there's no harm in it. Though I can't remember that last time I gave meat to a Mouse. This isn't a trick question is it?

MOUSE: Trick?

BUTCHER: With a hidden camera and all that? (peers around and at audience)

MOUSE: Camera?

BUTCHER: Oh, don't pretend you're fooling the Butcher! Just to make sure you're on the up-and-up, maybe you'd better do something for me.

MOUSE: Anything! Anything at all!

BUTCHER: Go to the Baker and get me a loaf of fresh soda bread.

MOUSE: I'm already there! Oh, where is a Baker when you need one? (crosses left)

BUTCHER: Low-calorie, mind you. And no seeds. I hate seeds. (crosses to mid center) Spend a whole day picking bloody seeds out of your teeth...

(BAKER enters from left carrying a loaf of bread.)

MOUSE: Ah! Baker at twelve o'clock!
CHORUS: *(sings)*
    The Mousie leapt, and skittered away,
    Till she came to the Baker and thus did say:
MOUSE: Dear Baker…
BAKER: *(screams and jumps away)* Eeek! A Mouse! A Mouse! Help! Get away, get away!
MOUSE: Please! Don't be afraid! I've been sent by the Butcher.
BAKER: *(calms down)* The Butcher sent you?
MOUSE: Yes. He wants you to give me bread, so that I may give him bread, that he may give me meat, so that I may give Farmer meat, that Farmer may give me hay, that I may give Cow hay, that Cow may give me milk, that I may give Cat milk, that Cat may give me my tail back again!
BAKER: Could you repeat that? I didn't get it all the first time.
MOUSE: Ooohhhh! This is so exasperating! Listen, all I need from you is a loaf of bread! No seeds, please.
BAKER: Hmmm. Seeing as you've been so polite — for a Mouse — I think I can spare a loaf of seedless seven-grain. *(hands loaf to Mouse)* Here you go!
MOUSE: Thank you, thank you, thank you!

(As Chorus sings, Mouse runs to mid center and gives the loaf to Butcher, who gives drumstick to Mouse, who gives drumstick to Farmer, who gives a handful of hay to Mouse, who gives hay to Cow, who gives a milk car-ton to Mouse, who skips over to Cat and gives carton to Cat. MUSIC: "The Mousie Leapt, Reprise.")

CHORUS: *(sings)*
    The Mousie gave her bread to Butcher
    Who gave her meat

That she gave to Farmer
Who gave her hay
That she gave to Cow
Who gave her milk
That she gave to Cat
Who said:

CAT: Maiow!

MOUSE: Now, may I *please* have my tail back?

CAT: *(tosses tail to Mouse)* This old thing? Suit yourself, said the old woman as she kissed the cow. *(sucks milk through straw)*

MOUSE: *(to audience)* See what kind of attitude I have to put up with? Of course, they say it wasn't always like this — cats and mice at each other's throat. In fact, I heard a tale from the Congo about a time when a Cat and a Rat lived in perfect harmony on a beautiful island.

(RAT enters from left and adjusts his sunglasses.)

MOUSE: They had plenty to eat and nothing to do but lay in the shade and watch the ocean. But like most creatures, they weren't satisfied with the good life they had. They wanted more.

(Mouse exits right as Rat crosses to down right.)

CAT: Morning, Rat.

RAT: Morning, Cat.

CAT: Another beautiful day in paradise.

RAT: Yeh. Beautiful and boring.

CAT: Boring? What do you mean? This *is* paradise, isn't it?

RAT: How do you know it's not even more of a paradise over there? *(points to audience)*

CAT: On the mainland?

RAT: You're reading me loud and clear, my feline friend.

(puts arm around Cat, as they gaze into audience) Over on the mainland there are villages.

CAT: What happens in a village?

RAT: Cats get fed without having to climb trees and catch birds. Rats get fed without having to dig in the dirt for nuts and roots. It's easy street!

CAT: So how do we get there from here?

RAT: We make a boat from the root of that big manioc tree. Then we sail away into the sunset!

(Cat and Rat go to down center and sit next to each other, facing audience and making rowing motions.)

CAT: This manioc root makes a good boat, Rat.

RAT: You bet. It's sturdy and tastes good!

CAT: Hmmm, that reminds me...I'm hungry. What do we have to eat?

RAT: *(looks behind himself)* Let's see...we have...uhhhh... we have...

CAT: I'm sure hungry!

RAT: Uhhhh...let's see...*(looks desperately underneath himself)*

CAT: I'm really, really, *really* hungry! What's for supper!

RAT: Nothing. We apparently forgot to bring any food.

CAT: Apparently or actually?

RAT: Actually and completely. There is no food.

CAT: Ahhhh! We're in the middle of the ocean, miles away from land, and we have no food?

RAT: Well, if you want to put it *that* way...

CAT: How would *you* put it?

RAT: Basically, we're going to die. But don't panic.

CAT: If we don't panic, what do we do?

RAT: *(curls up on side)* I'm going to save my energy and go to sleep.

CAT: That's the best idea I've heard all day! *(curls up on side, facing away from Rat)*

(Cat begins to snore; Rat rises on elbow and speaks to audience.)

RAT: I just remembered something. This boat is made of manioc root. And manioc root is a food we Rats love very much. *(looks at sleeping Cat, then audience)* Shhhhh! I'll just nibble a little bit from the bottom of the boat.

(Rat leans over and mimes nibbling floor; Cat awakes groggily and looks over at Rat, who pretends to be asleep.)

CAT: Hmmm...I could swear I heard a very strange noise. Oh well...

(Cat lies back down and sleeps; Rat leans over and begins nibbling.)

RAT: Oh, this is so delicious!

(Cat awakes a little quicker, looks over at Rat, who pretends to be asleep.)

CAT: Where is that noise coming from? I must be delerious from hunger. Oh well...

(Cat lies back down and sleeps; Rat leans over and begins nibbling.)

RAT: Oh, yum-yum-yum-yum-yum...just another little bite...whoops!

(Rat falls backward; Cat startles awake.)

CAT: What's all the noise?
RAT: Noise? You mean the water rushing into the boat?

CAT: Water! Aiiieee! Where did *that* come from?

(Cat backs up, squats as if avoiding water.)

RAT: It appears there is a hole in the bottom of the boat.

CAT: A hole! Where did *that* come from?

RAT: It appears someone's tooth has eaten a hole through the manioc root.

CAT: A tooth! And where did— *(looks at Rat and suddenly comprehends)* You miserable, no-good, low-down—

RAT: Don't panic! This is not a time to panic!

CAT: Rat-faced...

RAT: Careful! I resemble that remark! Besides, this situation is not as bad as it looks.

CAT: Our situation? Let's review our situation. *You* talk me into leaving our island paradise, *you* forget to bring food, and — while *I* am starving — *you* eat a hole in our boat! Did I leave anything out?

RAT: Yes! We just sank! Swim for the shore!

(Cat and Rat roll over several times and mime swimming; they crawl back to down center, panting.)

RAT: That was a healthy swim!

CAT: I'm going to eat you. Every last morsel.

RAT: I deserve it, my friend. But I am too wet now. I'd only give you indigestion. Let me dry off a bit, and then I'll be worth eating.

(Cat and Rat move apart and begin drying themselves; Cat is so busy drying himself, he does not notice Rat moving toward stool and making digging motions. After a few seconds Cat concludes drying himself and turns to Rat.)

CAT: Hey there, Rat! Are you ready for me to come eat you?

RAT: I certainly am. Hope you like your dinner on the run!

CAT: Mrrrowwww!

(Cat chases Rat around stage, with Rat ducking under stool.)

RAT: How do you like my new little hole in the ground? I call it Chez Rat!

CAT: You will never get out of that hole alive! I will stay here and wait forever!

RAT: Squeak! Squeak!

CAT: Maiow! Maiow!

RAT: Squeak! Squeak!

CAT: Maiow! Maiow!

RAT: Squeak! Squeak!

CAT: Maiow! Maiow!

(Mouse enters from right and scurries to down center.)

MOUSE: From that day on, these two creatures who had been best friends, became worst enemies. And today there is not a Cat in the whole world who is so fast asleep, he doesn't hear the chewing of a Rat. And there is not a Rat in the whole world who, when he sleeps in his hole, doesn't know there is a Cat waiting for him outside.

(LIGHTS OUT BRIEFLY; Cat and Rat exit right; Mouse remains at down center; LION enters from left and lies stretched out asleep at down left. LIGHTS UP FULL.)

MOUSE: Probably the best teller of tales in the entire history of tale-telling was a man named Aesop. He lived in Greece over twenty-five hundred years ago. And one of his favorite tales was about a Lion... *(points to Lion)* and a Mouse *(points to herself)*.

(Mouse pulls out kazoo and starts playing "Old MacDonald Had a Farm," strutting and enjoying herself immensely. Lion awakes, sees what is happening, and roars angrily.)

LION: Rowwwrrrrr!

(Mouse stops playing.)

MOUSE: I don't think that's quite how the tune goes.

LION: Rowwwrrrrr! *(rises and approaches Mouse)*

MOUSE: Fine, you take the next solo.

LION: Silence! *(grabs kazoo)* You've disturbed the sleep of the Lion — King of Beasts!

MOUSE: Weren't you the party who asked for an early wakeup call?

LION: I am going to eat you, little Mouse! Prepare to die! *(grabs Mouse by arm)*

MOUSE: Wait! Wait! Kind sir, please let me go! *(kneels)*

LION: Let you go! *(laughs heartily)* Ha-ha-ha-ha! Why would the Lion — King of Beasts — let you go?

MOUSE: Well, because, let's see, ummm, I know there's a reason, quick-quick, yes-yes, it's on the tip of my tongue, just a moment, I have a reason, there is a reason, ummm, yes-yes, I—

LION: *(raises paw as if to swat Mouse)* Rowwwrrrrr!

MOUSE: I've got it! Because someday I will repay you for your kindness!

LION: *(laughs heartily)* Ha-ha-ha-ha! That's your reason?

MOUSE: It's a good reason!

LION: It's the silliest thing the Lion — King of Beasts — has ever heard! The very idea of such an insignificant little creature as *you* ever being able to do anything useful for the mighty Lion — King of Beasts — is of great amusement. Ha-ha-ha-ha! Why, it is to make the Lion — King of Beast — laugh out loud. Ha-ha-ha-ha!

MOUSE: So, you're considering it?

LION: *(releases Mouse)* Yes, yes, run along little Mousie. You have afforded the Lion — King of Beasts — a good day's chuckle. Ha-ha-ha-ha!

(Mouse scampers off right; Lion settles back down asleep at down left. TWO HUNTERS enter stealthily from right, cross to the Lion and throw a net over him.)

LION: Rowwwrrrrr!

(Lion struggles but fails to escape; Hunters walk around and inspect him.)

HUNTER #1: Nice pussycat, nice little pussycat!

HUNTER #2: This is the biggest catch we've made all day! He'll fetch a good price at the bazaar.

HUNTER #1: Let's check our other traps. We'll come back for this one later.

HUNTER #2: Right. *(tugs on net)* This baby's not going anywhere.

(Hunters exit left; Lion moans for a few seconds, then notices he has the Mouse's kazoo. He toots a couple notes. Mouse peeks out from right.)

MOUSE: I thought I heard music…

(Lion toots again; Mouse walks nonchalantly across stage.)

MOUSE: Well, it *sounds* like music. *(to audience)* But it's not awfully good, is it?

(Lion toots again; Mouse sees him and acts exaggeratedly surprised.)

MOUSE: My goodness! It is a concert being given by the Lion —
(eggs audience to say it with her) King of Beasts!

LION: Please help me.

MOUSE: Help? You certainly do need help! For starters,
you're holding that instrument entirely wrong. And
you're counting the rhythm too quickly. (raises arms
like a conductor) Let's take it from the top, slowwwwly
and with expression!

LION: Rowwwrrrrr!

(Mouse jumps back.)

LION: Look, Mouse, I need your help. I'm sorry... about
before.

MOUSE: Sorry?

LION: Yes, sorry. Is that good enough?

MOUSE: Not quite. Say, "I am sorry for being a pompous
ninny."

LION: I am sorry for being a pompous ninny.

MOUSE: "I am sorry for having a rude and vulgar sense of
humor."

LION: I am sorry for having a rude and vulgar sense of
humor.

MOUSE: And I promise to *never* use that stupid, *stupid*
phrase "Lion — King of Beasts."

(Lion scowls, does not reply.)

MOUSE: Promise!

LION: All right, I promise!

MOUSE: Fine. I'll gnaw on these ropes with my sharp teeth
and have you free in a jiffy.

(Mouse gnaws on ropes, Lion tosses net aside and
rises.)

LION: Thank you, Mouse. You have taught a very important lesson to the Lion—

MOUSE: Watch it!

LION: To the Lion — King of the Kazoo! *(toots kazoo loudly as if roaring)*

(Mouse and Lion shake hands; Entire Cast comes onstage and sings "We Can Make Our Friendship Strong.")

ENTIRE CAST: *(sings)*
Now it's time to leave you;
We hope you've listened well.
For the stories we have told you
Were meant to ring a bell.

Cats and mice all over the world
Can't seem to get along.
But you and I can learn from them
And make our friendship strong.

(chorus)
We can make our friendship strong
By helping one another.
We can make our friendship strong
By showing that we care.
We can make our friendship strong
By smiling on our neighbor.
We can make our friendship strong
And make this world a paradise.

(LIGHTS OUT.)

THE END

The Mousie Leapt — verse
(words & music by L.E. McCullough)

♩ = 120

The   Mous-ie   leapt,   and   skitt-ered   a-   way,   till   she

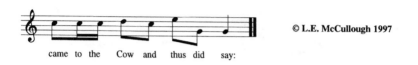

© L.E. McCullough 1997

came   to   the   Cow   and   thus   did   say:

The Mousie Leapt — reprise
(words & music by L.E. McCullough)

♩ = 120

The   Mous-ie   gave   her   bread   to   Butch-er,   who

gave   her   meat   that   she   gave   to   Far-   mer   who

gave   her   hay   that   she   gave   to   Cow   who

gave   her   milk   that   she   gave   to   Cat   who   said: *(Cat)* Mai-ow!

© L.E. McCullough 1997

Old MacDonald Had a Farm
(traditional, arranged by L.E. McCullough)

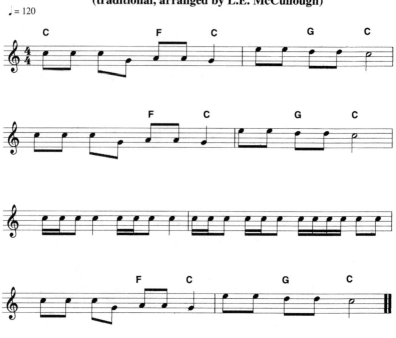

We Can Make Our Friendship Strong
(words & music by L.E. McCullough)

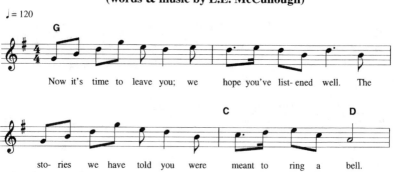

Now it's time to leave you; we hope you've list-ened well. The

sto- ries we have told you were meant to ring a bell.

We Can Make Our Friendship Strong, pg. 2

© L.E. McCullough 1997

Three Tales for Thrippence

Three is an important number in the religions and mythology of cultures around the world, from the Three Kings who visit the Baby Jesus to the Three Heavens of Taoism to the Three Warrior Goddesses of ancient Ireland — to name but three well-known examples. In fairy tales, nearly everything seems to happen in "threes," a fact some scholars have ascribed to a nearly universal human belief in the number three as a symbol of completion or perfection. See how many threes you can spot in these three tales from Spain (*The Three Wishes*), Papua (*The Three Sisters*) and England (*The Three Sillies*)...starting with the three sentences that make up this paragraph!

RUNNING TIME: 20 minutes

PLACE: Where Else But Fairy Land?

CAST: 23 actors, min. 7 boys, 11 girls

Grandmother	Bobby
Benny	Becky
Old Man	Old Woman
The Fairy Fortunata	Gata, the Cat
Perro, the Dog	3 Sisters
Snake	Farmer
Farmer's Wife	Farmer's Daughter
Gentleman	Cottage Woman
Cow	Traveler
3 Townsfolk	

STAGE SET: a chair at down right; a table and chair at down left

PROPS: three pennies, pot, spoon, large black pudding*, magic wand, 3 fishing sticks, 3 reed baskets, pitcher, loop of string, pair of boots, rake

EFFECTS: Sound — thunderclap; wind whistling and rain falling

MUSIC: *The Three-Penny Pig*

COSTUMES: Grandmother, Bobby, Benny and Becky wear contemporary casual dress; Other Humans wear simple medieval peasant clothes, except for Gentleman who dresses a bit fancier with a plumed hat, a jeweled necklace, bright sash; Fairy Fortunata wears a ballerina-type outfit spinkled with glitter and gold and silver with a white veil and a gold or silver wand; Cow, Snake, Dog and Cat wear appropriate animals masks and body coverings

* this can be a plastic or rubber item bought at a novelty shop or made at home; with a piece of velcro attached it can be stuck to the Old Woman's nose

---

(LIGHTS UP RIGHT on GRANDMOTHER and BOBBY, BECKY and BENNY at down right; Grandmother sits in a chair, with her grandchildren seated at her feet. They sing. MUSIC: "The Three-Penny Pig.")

ALL: *(sing)*
I went to the fair at Dungannon
And bought a three-penny pig.
I carried it home in my apron
While dancing a swaggering jig.

BOBBY: Grandmother, what's a "three-penny pig?"

GRANDMOTHER: In Ireland and the United Kingdom, they have a small silver coin called a "three-pence." It's worth three pennies. Or, as they sometimes say, a "thrippence."

BECKY: So the pig cost three cents!

GRANDMOTHER: That's right, Becky.

BENNY: Gosh, a whole pig for just three pennies!

GRANDMOTHER: You can get some very good deals in folk tales, Benny.

BOBBY: Grandmother, will you tell us a folk tale?

GRANDMOTHER: Oh, now, it's pretty late. Isn't it time for you children to be getting to bed?

BECKY: Please, Grandmother! Tell us a tale. Here's a penny! *(holds up a penny)*

BENNY: I'll give a penny, too! *(holds up a penny)*

BOBBY: Me, three! *(holds up a penny)*

BECKY: Tell a tale for each of us!

BENNY: Three tales for thrippence!

GRANDMOTHER: *(collects the pennies, chuckles)* All right, then. Once upon a time, on a cold winter's night long, long ago in a little village in Spain, there lived an Old Man and an Old Woman.

(LIGHTS UP LEFT on a table and chair at down left; OLD MAN sits on chair, OLD WOMAN holds a pot and stirs it with a spoon. GATA, the Cat, and PERRO, the Dog, lie on the floor to the right, sleeping.)

GRANDMOTHER: Now this old couple were really rather comfortable and wanted for nothing in the way of material goods. But instead of being grateful for their blessings, they envied the good things possessed by their neighbors.

OLD MAN: *(pounds table)* I was passing by Diego Mendoza's farm this morning. How I wish we had a fine house and farm like his!

OLD WOMAN: Aye, his house and farm are all right. *I* would like to live in a mansion such as that of Doña Isabella.

OLD MAN: And that old donkey of ours! Diego Mendoza's donkey is much better! Would that I owned a fine strong mule like that!

OLD WOMAN: No donkey for me! I should like a white horse with beautiful silk of scarlet and gold!

OLD MAN: Instead of fine animals, we have a silly old cat!

GATA: *(raises head)* Mrrrowww!

OLD WOMAN: And a lazy old dog!

PERRO: *(raises head)* Woooff!

(Gata and Perro go back to sleep and remain asleep until after second wish.)

OLD MAN: Some people have all the luck! They get whatever they wish for!

OLD WOMAN: Would that we had only to speak our wishes — and they would come true!

(LIGHTS FLICKER OFF AND ON. THE FAIRY FORTUNATA enters from right and twirls to down center. LIGHTS UP CENTER AND LEFT.)

OLD MAN: A beautiful woman has burst forth from the fireplace!

OLD WOMAN: Who-who-who are you?

FORTUNATA: I am the Fairy Fortunata! I have heard your complaints and have come to give you what you desire. Three wishes you shall have. One for you, Old Woman. *(waves wand at Old Woman)* One for you, Old Man. *(waves wand at Old Man)* And a third that you must agree upon together. *(waves wand twice)* There! May your restless hearts find contentment at last!

(LIGHTS FLICKER OFF AND ON as Fortunata twirls offstage right.)

OLD MAN: Three wishes! Oh, I can be *very* content with *my* wish! I think I will use it to be as prosperous as Diego Mendoza. No more, no less!

OLD WOMAN: But think, dear husband, would it not be wonderful to live in a palace? Domes and spires filled with rubies and sapphires…walls and ceilings and court-yards gleaming with gold and silver! Why, there are just so many things to wish for!

OLD MAN: It is obvious we cannot agree. Let us decide tomorrow.

OLD WOMAN: Fine. We will talk of other things besides wishes.

(They do not speak for several seconds as Old Man twiddles thumbs and Old Woman stirs spoon around in pot.)

OLD MAN: I passed by Diego Mendoza's house this morning. His wife was making black puddings. They smelled so good!

OLD WOMAN: Yes, indeed! They are delightful. Why, I wish I had one of Diego's black puddings in my pot this very minute!

(LIGHTS FLICKER OFF AND ON.)

OLD WOMAN: Oh no! *(pulls a black pudding from pot)*

OLD MAN: Look what you have done! You used up one of our wishes for a black pudding! You greedy creature! Why, I wish that silly pudding were stuck to your nose!

(LIGHTS FLICKER OFF AND ON; black pudding is stuck to Old Woman's nose.)

OLD WOMAN: *(screams, drops pot)* Aiiiieeee!

OLD MAN: I do not believe it! The pudding is stuck to your nose!

OLD WOMAN: *(unsuccessfully tries to pull pudding from nose)* Do not just stand there! Help me get this pudding off my nose!

(Gata and Perro rise and begin wailing and barking at the Old Woman, who jumps up on the chair.)

GATA: Maiow! Maiow! Maiow! Maiow!

PERRO: Woof! Woof! Woof! Woof!

OLD WOMAN: The cat and dog are trying to eat my nose! Get this pudding off me!

OLD MAN: Lie down on the table!

(Old Woman lies on her back on the table as Old Man stands on chair and unsuccessfully tries to pull pudding from nose and Gata and Perro wail and bark.)

OLD MAN: Andale, Gata! Andale, Perro!

(Gata and Perro cease wailing and barking and lie down.)

OLD WOMAN: These animals are going to eat my nose! Oh, husband, we must use the third wish to take it off!

OLD MAN: Are you mad? What of the new farm I wanted? And your new palace?

OLD WOMAN: I will never agree to wish for them!

OLD MAN: But let us wish for a case of precious jewels! And you can use them to cover your nose!

OLD WOMAN: No!

OLD MAN: Then, we will be left just as we were before!

OLD WOMAN: That is all I ask! I see now that we had all we needed!

OLD MAN: Very well. Let us make the third wish.

(Old Man and Old Woman stand and face audience.)

OLD MAN & OLD WOMAN: Dear Fortunata, do hear us implore; we wish only to be as we were before!

(LIGHTS FLICKER OFF AND ON, THEN OFF; Old Man, Old Woman, Gata, Perro exit left.)

GRANDMOTHER: And, lo and behold — their third wish was granted!

(Grandmother, Bobby, Becky and Benny sing. MUSIC: "The Three-Penny Pig.")

ALL: *(sing)*
    If you ever have three wishes,
    You'd better watch what you say.
    Don't be greedy and selfish,
    Or you'll wish all your luck away.

(LIGHTS UP CENTER AND LEFT. A SNAKE is coiled up in a ball at down center, sitting on floor, head down between knees.)

GRANDMOTHER: Way back in the time when animals could talk, three Sisters lived in the tropical jungle of Papua near the Coral Sea. One day, they went down to the sea to fish. The eldest Sister went down first to get the best fishing spot.

(SISTER #1 enters from left carrying a fishing stick and basket; she sees Snake and stops, irritated.)

SISTER #1: Why, it is a Snake! Snake, you are blocking my path! Get out of the way!

SNAKE: *(lifts head but remains coiled)* Dear girl, I am so

very hungry. Can you give me a small bit of the food you carry in your hand?

SISTER #1: Give food to a Snake? That I will never do! Let me pass!

(Snake lowers head and Sister #1 tromps around Snake, crossing to mid center, where she stands, her fishing stick cast forward as if fishing.)

GRANDMOTHER: A short while later, the second Sister came walking along the path.

(SISTER #2 enters from left carrying a fishing stick and basket; she sees Snake and stops, irritated.)

SISTER #2: Snake, you are blocking my path! Get out of the way!

SNAKE: *(lifts head but remains coiled)* Dear girl, I am so very, very hungry. Can you give me a small bit of the food you carry in your hand?

SISTER #2: Give food to a Snake? That I will never do! Let me pass!

(Snake lowers head and Sister #2 tromps around Snake, crossing to mid center, where she stands next to Sister #1, her fishing stick cast forward as if fishing.)

GRANDMOTHER: Right after that, the youngest Sister came walking along the path.

(SISTER #3 enters from left carrying a fishing stick and basket; she sees Snake and stops.)

SISTER #3: Why, it is a Snake! And it looks quite sad!

SNAKE: *(lifts head but remains coiled)* Dear girl, I am so

very, very, *very* hungry. Can you perhaps give me just a small bit of the food you carry in your hand?

SISTER #3: Why, certainly, you poor creature! *(mimes handing him food)*

SNAKE: That is very good. And you are very kind. Where are you going?

SISTER #3: I am going to the sea to fish.

SNAKE: I have lived in this jungle many, many years. And I can tell you many, many things. When you hear a loud noise in the sky like thunder, begin to fish. When you hear that noise a second time, climb the hill behind you.

SISTER #3: Your words puzzle me, Snake. But thank you for sharing them with me. I will do as you say.

(Snake lowers head and Sister #3 walks gently around Snake, crossing to mid center, where she stands next to Sister #2; Sister #3 holds her fishing stick on her shoulder.)

SISTER #3: Greetings, my Sisters. How are you this fine day?

SISTER #1: Terrible! I have caught no fish at all.

SISTER #2: I think it is the fault of that Snake we met along the path. He has put a jinx upon us. We might as well go home.

(SOUND: thunderclap offstage. Sisters #1 and 2 cringe and take a step backward, but Sister #3 calmly casts out her fishing stick and begins to fish; Sisters #1 and 2 laugh.)

SISTER #1: Look, our youngest Sister has begun fishing!

SISTER #2: She must have lost her wits!

SISTER #1: Sister, do not waste your time! There are no fish here today!

SISTER #3: Snake told me to begin fishing when I first heard thunder.

(Sisters #1 and 2 laugh; Sister #3 mimes reeling in lots of fish and putting them in her basket.)

SISTER #2: Snake told her! *(laughs)*
SISTER #1: Our youngest Sister believes the words of a reptile! *(laughs)*

(Sisters #1 and 2 notice Sister #3 is catching fish; they stop laughing.)

SISTER #2: Look! Our youngest Sister is catching many fish!
SISTER #1: Why, her basket is nearly full!
SISTER #2: Let us stay and fish then!

(Sisters #1 and 2 cast out fishing sticks; SOUND: thunderclap offstage. Sister #3 collects basket and scurries to mid left, kneels and covers her head, as Sisters #1 and 2 continue fishing.)

SISTER #1: What can be wrong with her? Did you see the way she ran up that hill?
SISTER #2: Silly girl! She has been out in the sun too long!

(Sisters #1 and 2 laugh and continue fishing. SOUND: wind whistling and rain falling. Sisters #1 and 2 look up above.)

SISTER #1: A huge storm is coming!
SISTER #2: A terrible rain is falling!
SISTER #1: The river is rising!
SISTER #2: We will be swept out to sea!

(Sisters #1 and 2 cower in fear. LIGHTS FLICKER OFF AND ON SEVERAL TIMES as SOUND of storm increases,

then fades. Sisters #1 and 2 sink to floor and roll away to up center and lie still.)

SISTERS #1 & 2: Help! Help, us Sister! We are drowning! Helllllllppp!

(Sister #3 raises her head, stands and crosses slowly to down center.)

SNAKE: *(raises head)* Greetings, kind girl. Did you catch many fish?

SISTER #3: Yes, Snake. I caught many fish. But I fear my Sisters have been swept out to sea and drowned!

SNAKE: That is very sad. If they had given me food when I asked, they would have heard me tell of the two thunderclaps. And they would now be eating fish, instead of being eaten by them. *(smiles, lowers head)*

(SOUND: thunderclap offstage. LIGHTS OUT. Grandmother, Bobby, Becky and Benny sing. MUSIC: "The Three-Penny Pig.")

ALL: *(sing)*
    The next time somebody asks you
    To give them a wee bit of help,
    Be sure to listen politely,
    Or you might be swallowing kelp.

GRANDMOTHER: Once upon a time, in merry old England, there lived a Farmer, his Wife and their Daughter.

(LIGHTS UP CENTER AND LEFT on FARMER, FARMER'S WIFE and FARMER'S DAUGHTER gathered around table at down left. A pitcher sits on the table.)

GRANDMOTHER: The Daughter had just met a fine, handsome Gentleman in town that day, and at six o'clock he came to visit.

(GENTLEMAN enters from down right, crosses stage and mimes knocking on door.)

GENTLEMAN: Knock, knock, knock!
FARMER: Who's there?
GENTLEMAN: It is I, a Gentleman of the town.
WIFE: A Gentleman to see our Daughter! Come in! Come in!
GENTLEMAN: *(to audience)* A full purse never lacks friends!

(Gentleman enters, is greeted with great fuss by Farmer and Wife and given the seat at the table.)

WIFE: Daughter, you run to the stable and get the milk for dinner.
DAUGHTER: Yes, mum. *(curtseys, takes pitcher and crosses to down center)*
GRANDMOTHER: While the Daughter was in the stable drawing the milk, she chanced to look up at the ceiling. *(Daughter gazes upward.)*

GRANDMOTHER: And there she saw a mallet stuck in one of the beams.

(Daughter walks around in a circle staring upward.)

DAUGHTER: Why, I have never noticed that mallet stuck up there in the beam! *(to audience)* You know, it is very dangerous for that mallet to be hanging there like that! Suppose that Gentleman and I was to fall in love and then be married…And suppose we was to have ourselves a son…And suppose that son was to grow up to be a man…And suppose one day he was to come to the stable like as I am now — and that mallet was to come loose from the beam and fall on his tender little head! Oh, the pain! The pain!

(Daughter sits and sobs loudly.)

FARMER: I say, Wife, what is keeping our Daughter? She has been in the stable for near a quarter hour!

GENTLEMAN: Oh, no rush, no rush! Always remember: haste makes waste! The ripest fruit falls first! Two swallows do not a summer make!

FARMER: *(to Wife)* Odd sort of chap, for a Gentleman.

WIFE: Husband, go and see about our Daughter right away!

(Farmer crosses to down center and sees Daughter sobbing.)

FARMER: Daughter, whatever is the matter?

DAUGHTER: Oh, Father, look at that dreadful horrid mallet! *(points upward)*

FARMER: *(looks upward)* That mallet sticking in the beam? Why, it is just an ordinary mallet! What is so dreadful and horrid about it?

DAUGHTER: *(sobs)* Oh, Father, suppose me and the Gentleman was to fall in love and then be married. And then have ourselves a son, and he grow up to be a man, and one day he was to come to the stable like as we are now — and that mallet was to come loose from the beam and fall on his tender little head! Oh, the pain! The pain!

(Daughter sobs loudly; Farmer sits next to her.)

FARMER: Now, now, Daughter. That would indeed be a dreadful horrid thing. Yes, that would be a *very* dreadful horrid thing. *(sniffles)* My own little grandson...struck in his tender head with a dreadful horrid mallet!

(Farmer sobs loudly along with Daughter.)

WIFE: It has been near a quarter hour since my husband's been gone. And this fine Gentleman waiting for his supper!

GENTLEMAN: Patience is a flower that grows not in every garden.

WIFE: Yes. Perhaps something is amiss in the stable! Begging your pardon, I will see.

(Wife crosses to down center, followed by Gentleman, and sees Daughter and Father sobbing; Wife shakes Daughter.)

WIFE: Daughter! Where is the pitcher of milk you were sent for?

DAUGHTER: Oh, mother, look above! *(points upward)*

WIFE: *(looks upward)* The pitcher of milk is up there? All I see is a mallet!

FARMER: Yes, and suppose our Daughter was to marry the Gentleman and then they have themselves a son, and he grow up to be a man that one day come to the stable seeking to fill his pitcher of milk and — *pow!* That mallet smack down full hard on his tender little head!

(Father and Daughter sob loudly; Mother sits next to them and begins sobbing, too.)

WIFE: Oh, the pain! The pain!

GENTLEMAN: What incredible silliness! I believe you three are the biggest sillies in all of England! *(turns to exit left)*

WIFE: Where are you going? Don't you want to marry our Daughter?

GENTLEMAN: That silly creature? Madam, I shall travel around the country, and when I meet three bigger sillies than you three, then and only then shall I return and marry your Daughter!

FARMER: And not a moment too soon!

(Farmer, Wife and Daughter wave goodbye to Gentleman who exits left; they follow him a few seconds after; Gentleman returns onstage from left and walks up left and to mid center.)

GRANDMOTHER: The Gentleman went on his way round the country, and he saw a good many silly things. Yet, he did not see a bigger silly until he came upon a woman trying to push a cow up a ladder onto the top of her cottage.

(A COTTAGE WOMAN and COW enter from right; the Cottage Woman pushes the cow from behind to down center, where the Cow refuses to move further.)

COTTAGE WOMAN: Come on, Bessie! Go up the ladder! That's a good girl! Just…go…up…the…ladder!

COW: *(distressed)* Mooooooo!

GENTLEMNAN: I say there, madam! Why are you trying to push that cow up the ladder?

COTTAGE WOMAN: There is a patch of delicious grass growing on the roof of the cottage. I want my cow to eat it. I know she will like it very much.

COW: *(distressed)* Mooooooo!

COTTAGE WOMAN: And she will be quite safe! *(shows loop of string)* I will tie this loop of string around her neck and pass it down through the chimney. I will tie the string to my wrist as I go about my chores. If she falls off the roof, I will know about it right away.

GENTLEMAN: Oh, you poor, poor silly! Why don't *you* climb the ladder onto the roof, cut the grass and throw it down to the cow?

COTTAGE WOMAN: *(chuckles)* Young man, you must be joking! Everyone knows that grass always tastes better when eaten on the roof!

COW: *(distressed)* Mooooooo!
GENTLEMAN: *(to audience)* That is one very big silly!

(Cottage Woman pushes Cow offstage left. Gentleman walks up right and back to down center. A TRAVELER [in socks] enters from right carrying a pair of boots; at down center he puts them on the floor, shakes hands with the Gentleman, then backs up a few feet to the right and turns and faces the boots.)

GRANDMOTHER: The Gentleman went on from there, and later stopped for the night at a country inn. The man who shared his room was a Traveler, who seemed at first glance to be a very pleasant fellow. But when they both awoke in the morning, the Gentleman saw a very surprising thing.

(Traveler races forward and attempts to jump into the boots; he fails and falls flat.)

GENTLEMAN: My good sir, what is the matter?
TRAVELER: *(picks himself up and walks back to where he started his run)* Blasted boots! I think boots are the most awkward things ever worn! I cannot think what sort of scoundrel invented them!

(Traveler races forward and attempts to jump into the boots; he fails and falls flat.)

TRAVELER: *(picks himself up)* My curse upon you, boots! Why, do you know it takes me the best part of an hour every morning to get into the confounded things? However do you get into yours?
GENTLEMAN: *(to audience)* That is another *very* big silly! *(to Traveler)* Sir, step this way, please!

(Gentleman picks up boots and leads Traveler to chair at down left, where Traveler sits and Gentleman puts boots on his feet. Traveler exits left; Gentleman walks up left then back to down left. THREE TOWNSFOLK enter from right and stand at down center; SPOTLIGHT SHINES DOWN CENTER. TOWNSFOLK #1 carries a rake and begins raking the stage, as if trying to rake up the spotlight.)

GRANDMOTHER: The next day the Gentleman continued his travels searching for sillies. He came to a village where a crowd of people stood round a pond. They held rakes and hoes and brooms and pitchforks, which they dipped into the water.

GENTLEMAN: My goodness, someone must be drowning! Citizens, what is the matter?

TOWNSFOLK #1: Matter enough! The moon has fallen into the pond!

TOWNSFOLK #2: We must get it out!

TOWNSFOLK #3: If the moon stays in the water much longer, it will drown!

GENTLEMAN: *(laughs)* Ha-ha-ha! Good people, look up in the sky!

(Townsfolk look upward.)

GENTLEMAN: See? The moon is still in the sky! What you see in the water is the reflection of the moon!

(Townsfolk look at spotlight on floor, then up again, then back at floor.)

TOWNSFOLK #1: *(points at floor)* Well, that is *part* of the moon anyway!

TOWNSFOLK #2: And it is still caught in the pond!

TOWNSFOLK #3: Quick, we must get it out!

(Townsfolk rake furiously at spotlight on floor as Gentleman strolls to down left.)

GENTLEMAN: *(to audience) That* is the biggest bunch of sillies I have *ever* seen!

(Gentleman exits left, followed by Townsfolk as LIGHTS FADE OUT, THEN QUICKLY UP on Grandmother, Bobby, Becky and Benny at down right.)

BOBBY: Did the Gentleman marry the Farmer's Daughter?

GRANDMOTHER: Oh, yes. He had found three bigger sillies.

BECKY: Did they live happily ever after?

GRANDMOTHER: Yes, and they had many silly children who had many, many silly grandchildren.

BENNY: That would be us!

GRANDMOTHER: And you would be ready for bedtime! One more song and off you go!

(Grandmother, Bobby, Becky and Benny begin singing; Entire Cast enters and joins on second verse. MUSIC: "The Three-Penny Pig.")

GRANDMOTHER, BOBBY, BECKY & BENNY: *(sing)*
Three sisters, three wishes, three sillies;
Three tales we told about threes.
And if you pay us a thrippence,
You may tell them whenever you please.

ENTIRE CAST: *(sing)*
I went to the fair at Dungannon
And bought a three-penny pig.
I carried it home in my apron
While dancing a swaggering jig.

(LIGHTS OUT.)

THE END

The Three-Penny Pig

(traditional, arranged by L.E. McCullough)

I went to the fair at Dun- gan- non and bought a three- pen- ny pig. I car- ried it home in my a- pron while dan- cing a swagg- er- ing jig.

The Twelve Months

The plucky heroine of this Slovakian tale, a variant of the popular Cinderalla legend, must contend with not only an evil step-mother but an equally nasty step-sister! Psychologist Bruno Bettelheim believes that the prevalent use of the evil step-mother and step-sibling figures in fairy tales throughout the world reflects the natural anger and confusion a child occasionally feels toward its parents during the course of growing up; by creating a "pseudo-family" of "imposters" (these awful people can't be my *real* family!), the child can express negative emotions without losing its overall sense of security and trust within the family unit. Like the best fairy tales, *The Twelve Months* teaches an important lesson — polite people eventually succeed in life and live happily ever after; rude people spend their lives wandering in the cold.

RUNNING TIME: 15 minutes

PLACE: Slovakia

CAST: 17 actors, min. 3 boys, 5 girls

Narrator	Old Woman
Dobrunka	Katinka
12 Months	Prince

STAGE SET: table and 2 chairs at down left; a bonfire at mid center; a platform or riser at up center

PROPS: broom, staff, bunch of violets, basket of strawberries, 2 apples, wedding ring

EFFECTS: Sound — wind whistling

COSTUMES: Narrator can wear contemporary dress or the traditional garb of other characters; Dobrunka wears a peasant blouse and skirt, a bonnet, stockings and slippers; Katinka and Old Woman wear slovenly, ill-fitting clothes with their hair disheveled; Prince dresses as an aristocrat; each of the 12 Months wears a robe, hood, and mantle — December, January and February are white, March, April and May are green, June, July and August are gold; September, October and November are purple; January has long white beard and carries a staff

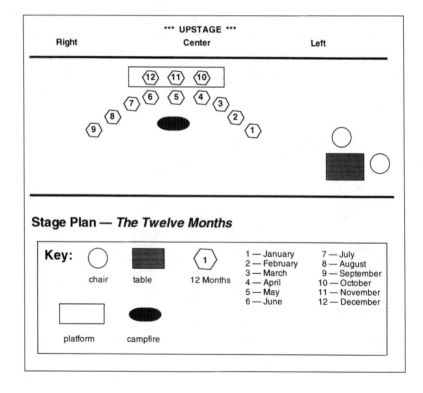

Stage Plan — *The Twelve Months*

(SPOTLIGHT ON NARRATOR at down right; LIGHTS UP LEFT on OLD WOMAN, KATINKA and DOBRUNKA at down left; Old Woman and Katinka sit at table; Dobrunka stands behind them, holding a broom.)

NARRATOR: *(to audience)* Once upon a time — a long, long time ago — there were three women who lived in a tiny cottage high in the Tatra Mountains of Slovakia. One was an Old Woman—

OLD WOMAN: *(shouts, pounds table)* Dobrunka!

NARRATOR: The second was her daughter, Katinka—

KATINKA: *(shouts, pounds table)* Dobrunka!

NARRATOR: And the third was a foster child, Dobrunka.

DOBRUNKA: *(comes to table)* Here I am! How can I be of service?

NARRATOR: The Old Woman and her daughter, Katinka, were dreadfully cruel to Dobrunka. They treated her like a servant instead of a family member.

OLD WOMAN: Cook the supper!

KATINKA: Sweep the floor!

OLD WOMAN: Wash the laundry!

KATINKA: Spin the flax!

OLD WOMAN: Weave the wool!

KATINKA: Cut the grass!

OLD WOMAN: Milk the cow!

KATINKA: And don't forget to make my bed!

DOBRUNKA: Yes, mother; yes, sister! I will gladly do these chores to make our home a happy one!

(Dobrunka sweeps with renewed vigor.)

NARRATOR: Poor Dobrunka worked very hard, and she never said a cross word in reply. Naturally, her unceasing sweetness made the Old Woman and Katinka even angrier.

KATINKA: *(to Old Woman)* I cannot stand that girl any longer! She is so nice, I want to scream!

OLD WOMAN: I have an idea. Listen…*(whispers in Katinka's ear as Katinka nods)*

(Katinka stands and approaches Dobrunka.)

NARRATOR: And so it was that on a very cold day in January, when the earth was frozen solid and the cottage window panes were covered with snow, Katinka called to Dobrunka.

KATINKA: *(mock-sweetly)* Oh, Dobrunka!

DOBRUNKA: Yes, my sister?

KATINKA: Don't you agree that violets are among the loveliest flowers in the world?

DOBRUNKA: Why, yes, my sister, violets are very lovely, indeed.

KATINKA: Well, I have taken a fancy for them. And I want you to go to the forest and bring me a bunch, so I may hold them close and smell their sweetness.

DOBRUNKA: But, sister, I cannot find violets on a day like today. All the forest flowers are buried under the snow.

KATINKA: You dare to contradict me? You ungrateful wretch! I command you to go to the forest and bring back a bunch of violets!

DOBRUNKA: But, sister, be reasonable!

OLD WOMAN: Silence! You will do as your sister asks, or you will never enjoy the hospitality of this house again!

DOBRUNKA: But, mother—

(Old Woman grabs Dobrunka by the arm and shoves her toward center.)

OLD WOMAN: Bring back violets for Katinka, or don't come back at all!

(LIGHTS OUT LEFT; SPOTLIGHT ON Dobrunka at down center as she peers anxiously about her and paces fretfully.)

NARRATOR: So poor Dobrunka wandered in the cold forest, without warm winter clothing or food. The ground was entirely covered with snow, with not a flower to be seen. Even the branches of the trees were blanketed with a thick coat of white. But Dobrunka was not a girl to give up hope.

(Dobrunka points out toward audience.)

DOBRUNKA: Is that a light? There on the mountain top! Shining and dancing in the distance, like the flame of a mighty fire! I must see!

(Dobrunka exits left; LIGHTS UP CENTER ON THE TWELVE MONTHS standing at mid and up center around a bonfire; Dobrunka re-enters from left and sees them.)

DOBRUNKA: This is an incredible sight! Twelve robed, hooded figures standing around a blazing fire! Why, they must be the spirits who govern the Twelve Months of the year! *(approaches JANUARY, who holds a staff)* My good sir January, I pray you permit me to warm myself by your fire. It is so very cold, and I will take only a little heat.
JANUARY: You may go to the fire. Then tell us why have you come to this place.
DOBRUNKA: I am looking for violets.
TWELVE MONTHS: Violets!

(The Twelve Months laugh.)

FEBRUARY: This is not the season for violets!

MARCH: What sort of a girl would look for violets in winter?

DOBRUNKA: Begging your pardon, good folk, I know this is not the season for violets. But my foster mother and sister thrust me out of doors and commanded me to find them. If I do not, they will never let me return.

JANUARY: Hmmm. Perhaps we can assist you. Sister April, I believe this is your business.

(APRIL takes the staff from January, goes to the fire and stirs it.)

DOBRUNKA: The flames arise, high into the sky! *(gazes around her)* And look, the snow is melting! Buds bloom on trees, grass turns green underfoot! Why, it is Spring! And there is a patch of violets! *(runs to down center and mimes picking violets)*

JANUARY: Make haste, child, and gather your violets.

DOBRUNKA: Thank you all very much! You have been so kind.

FEBRUARY: And because you have been courteous and polite, Sister April will provide you with a warm way home.

(April waves the staff toward down right; Dobrunka curtseys and walks to down right, picks up a bunch of violets from Narrator, then crosses back to down left.)

NARRATOR: And so Dobrunka returned to the house along a green sunny path that cut right through the frost and snow of the forest.

(LIGHTS OUT CENTER; LIGHTS UP LEFT on Old Woman and Katinka sitting at table.)

OLD WOMAN: Well, that is the last we will ever see of that troublesome Dobrunka.

KATINKA: I am sure she is making a good breakfast for the wolves!

(Old Woman and Katinka laugh; Dobrunka rushes up to them with a bunch of violets.)

DOBRUNKA: Mother, sister, see what I have found!

KATINKA: Violets! Where did you get them?

DOBRUNKA: On the mountain top. They lay like a beautiful blue carpet all through the forest.

KATINKA: *(snatches violets)* Liar! You could not have possibly found these in the forest!

OLD WOMAN: Never mind! I have a taste for fresh strawberries. Go to the forest and find some!

DOBRUNKA: But, mother, there are no strawberries under the snow.

OLD WOMAN: Hold your insolent tongue and do as I bid you!

(Old Woman grabs Dobrunka by the arm and shoves her toward center. LIGHTS OUT LEFT; SPOTLIGHT ON Dobrunka at down center as she peers anxiously about her and paces fretfully.)

NARRATOR: Once again poor Dobrunka set off through the cold forest. She spent hours searching for the light she had seen before. At last, when she had nearly perished with hunger and cold, she found it.

(LIGHTS UP CENTER ON THE TWELVE MONTHS standing at mid and up center; Dobrunka turns and approaches them.)

DOBRUNKA: My good sir January, I pray you permit me to

warm myself by your fire. It is so very cold, and I will take only a little heat.

JANUARY: You may go to the fire. Then tell us why have you come to this place again.

DOBRUNKA: I am looking for strawberries.

TWELVE MONTHS: Strawberries!

(The Twelve Months laugh.)

MAY: This is not the season for strawberries!

JULY: What sort of a girl would look for strawberries in winter?

DOBRUNKA: Begging your pardon, good folk, I know this is not the season for strawberries. But my foster mother and sister thrust me out of doors and commanded me to find them. If I do not, they will never let me return.

JANUARY: Hmmm. Perhaps we can assist you. Brother June, I believe this is your business.

(JUNE takes the staff from January, goes to the fire and stirs it.)

DOBRUNKA: The flames arise, high into the sky! *(gazes around her)* And look, the snow is melting! Birds sing and leaves fill the trees! Why, it is Summer! And there is a patch of ripe and luscious strawberries! *(runs to down center and mimes picking strawberries)*

JANUARY: Make haste, child, and gather your strawberries.

DOBRUNKA: Thank you all very much! You have been so kind.

AUGUST: And because you have been courteous and polite, Brother June will provide you with a warm way home.

(June waves the staff toward down right; Dobrunka curtseys and walks to down right, picks up a basket of strawberries from Narrator, then crosses back to down left.)

NARRATOR: And so Dobrunka returned to the house along a summery green path that cut right through the wintry heart of the forest.

(LIGHTS OUT CENTER; LIGHTS UP LEFT on Old Woman and Katinka sitting at table.)

OLD WOMAN: What a fool that Dobrunka is! She'll sooner find snow in July than strawberries in winter!

KATINKA: I am sure she is making a good supper for the bears!

(Old Woman and Katinka laugh; Dobrunka rushes up to them with a basket of strawberries.)

DOBRUNKA: Mother, sister, see what I have found!

KATINKA: Strawberries! Where did you get them?

DOBRUNKA: On the mountain top as before. They lay like a beautiful crimson carpet all through the forest.

KATINKA: *(snatches strawberries)* Liar! You could not have possibly found these in the forest!

OLD WOMAN: Never mind! I have a taste for some rosy red apples. Go to the forest and find some!

DOBRUNKA: But, mother, there are no apples in winter.

OLD WOMAN: Hold your insolent tongue and do as I bid you!

(Old Woman grabs Dobrunka by the arm and shoves her toward center. LIGHTS OUT LEFT; LIGHTS UP CENTER ON THE TWELVE MONTHS standing at mid and up center; Dobrunka approaches them.)

NARRATOR: This time Dobrunka went straight to the mountain top and found the Twelve Months gathered around the fire.

DOBRUNKA: My good folk, I beg your assistance once more.

My foster mother and sister have sent me to find rosy red apples.

TWELVE MONTHS: Apples!

(The Twelve Months laugh.)

OCTOBER: This is not the season for apples!

NOVEMBER: What sort of a girl would look for apples in winter?

JANUARY: Neveretheless, this girl is faithful and pure of heart. We must assist her. Madame September, I believe this is your business.

(SEPTEMBER takes the staff from January, goes to the fire and stirs it.)

DOBRUNKA: The flames arise, high into the sky! *(gazes around her)* And look, the snow is melting! It is autumn! And there is an apple tree! *(runs to down center and mimes shaking a tree and picking up two fallen apples.)*

JANUARY: There are two apples. Make haste, child, and gather them.

DOBRUNKA: Thank you all very much! You have been so kind.

DECEMBER: And because you have been courteous and polite, Madame September will provide you with a warm way home.

(September waves the staff toward down right; Dobrunka curtseys and walks to down right, picks up two apples from Narrator, then crosses back to down left.)

NARRATOR: And so Dobrunka returned to the house along a bright path of rich autumn color that cut right through the wintry heart of the forest.

(LIGHTS OUT CENTER; LIGHTS UP LEFT on Old Woman and Katinka sitting at table.)

OLD WOMAN: I believe my plan will work this time. Whoever she has been stealing from will surely punish her for good.

KATINKA: I am sure she is a midnight snack for the mountain vultures!

(Old Woman and Katinka laugh; Dobrunka rushes up to them with two apples.)

DOBRUNKA: Mother, sister, see what I have found!

KATINKA: Apples! Where did you get them? Oh, don't bother to answer! We are sick to death of your lies!

DOBRUNKA: But I am not lying! I saw a tree that was filled with rosy red apples.

KATINKA: And you brought only two! I am sure you ate all the rest!

OLD WOMAN: Never mind! My daughter and I will find this magic apple tree. And bring back a hundred apples all for ourselves.

DOBRUNKA: But you do not understand!

OLD WOMAN: Silence! Stay here and sweep the floor until we return!

DOBRUNKA: Yes, mother. I will gladly do these chores to make our home a happy one.

(Katinka makes an ugly face at Dobrunka, who silently picks up broom and begins sweeping. LIGHTS OUT LEFT; SPOTLIGHT ON Old Woman and Katinka at down center as they peer about. Katinka turns and points at mid center.)

KATINKA: Is that a light?

OLD WOMAN: Where?

KATINKA: On the mountain top!

(LIGHTS UP CENTER ON THE TWELVE MONTHS standing at mid and up center; Old Woman and Katinka approach them and swagger up to the fire.)

OLD WOMAN: Can't you make this fire any hotter? What sort of an inn is this, anyway?

KATINKA: We're freezing our toes off, and they just sit and stare at us! Dolts!

OLD WOMAN: Morons!

KATINKA: Idiots!

OLD WOMAN: Imbeciles!

KATINKA: Utter cretins!

OLD WOMAN: *(to January)* You, old geezer! Say something!

JANUARY: Why have you come to this place?

KATINKA: As if *our* business were any of *your* business! What a silly-looking bevy of lunatics! Let us be on our way, mother!

(Old Woman and Katinka turn and face audience; STAGE GOES DARK. SOUND: wind whistling.)

TWELVE MONTHS: Lunatics!

(The Twelve Months laugh; Old Woman and Katinka scream and exit right.)

OLD WOMAN & KATINKA: Aiieeee!

(LIGHTS UP LEFT on Dobrunka sweeping at down left; SPOTLIGHT ON Narrator at down right.)

NARRATOR: Dobrunka waited at home that night and for several days and nights after. But the Old Woman and Katinka did not come back. Dobrunka asked—

DOBRUNKA: I wonder what could have happened to my foster mother and sister?

(The Twelve Months laugh.)

NARRATOR: The only answer she received was the icy wind whistling through the trees...and the crackling of boughs snapping under their heavy burdens of snow.

(PRINCE enters from left and takes Dobrunka's hand, putting a ring on her finger.)

NARRATOR: Winter passed and spring and summer came, and as the Old Woman and Katinka never returned, Dobrunka became mistress of the cottage, the garden and the cow. In the course of time, she met a handsome Prince, and he and Dobrunka were married and lived very happily ever after.

PRINCE: My dearest Princess, what is thy favorite month of the year?

DOBRUNKA: My favorite month? Why, my sweet Prince, I love each and every one!

PRINCE: You have no favorite then?

DOBRUNKA: Perhaps January.

PRINCE: January? Pray tell why?

DOBRUNKA: No matter how bitter and icy its winds may blow, there are violets, strawberries and apples in the snow!

(LIGHTS OUT.)

THE END

Una and the Goblin King

This tale from Ireland is part of a long tradition of dragon-slayer tales — St. Michael, Hercules, St. George, King Arthur — except that the hero this time is a heroine and the dragon is a goblin! *Circumambulation* is a ceremonial walking around an object, place or person in the direction of the sun's movement across the sky that occurs all over the world; this is done to bring good luck and healing. *Widdershins* is walking the opposite way around the sun and is a device used by fairy tale sorcerers to make evil happen instead of good. *Una and the Goblin King* also includes a warning against eating food in the land of the dead, a motif found in tales as far apart in origin as New Guinea and New Zealand, North America and Europe and is perhaps best known in the ancient Greek myth of Persephone trapped in the underworld for eating one small pomegranate. A shillelagh is a carved stick popular in Ireland since the late 1700s, generally used for walking, occasionally for fighting goblins.

RUNNING TIME: 15 minutes

PLACE: Ireland

CAST: 12 actors, min. 3 boys, 4 girls

Una	Maeve
Queen Emer	Cormac, the Druid
Horseherd	Cowherd
Henwife	The Goblin King
4 Goblins	

STAGE SET: at mid left, a scrim with a drawing of a castle; at mid right, a stool with a gold or silver cloth over the seat

PROPS: ball, shillelagh, bowl, 5 swords

EFFECTS: Sound — wind whistling; horses neighing; cattle mooing; chickens cackling

COSTUMES: Humans wear medieval garb appropriate to status and occupation; Cormac the Druid can wear a long robe with hood; Goblins have hideous face masks

PERFORMANCE NOTE: when goblins, witches, trolls, etc. "burst apart" or die from rays of the sun or magic swords and so forth, they can fling confetti in the air to symbolize their dissolution into smithereens

---

(Children's laughter is heard for several seconds offstage left; laughter fades; SPOTLIGHT ON CORMAC THE DRUID standing down right, facing audience.)

CORMAC: I am Cormac, and I have lived in the green and pleasant land of Erin for many, many centuries. I belong to the order of men called "druids" — those who possess knowledge of mysterious, magical things. And the story I shall tell you today, is how a young girl named Una used magic to rescue her sister Maeve from the Goblin King of Elfland.

(SPOTLIGHT OUT; Cormac exits right; LIGHTS UP CENTER as UNA and MAEVE skip out from stage left to down center, laughing gaily and tossing a ball back and forth. When Una catches the ball, Maeve laughingly taunts her.)

UNA AND THE GOBLIN KING **155**

MAEVE: *(singsong)* I can throw farther than Una! I can throw farther than Una!

UNA: You cannot, Maeve! And I will prove it!

(Una rares back and heaves the ball offstage left; Una and Maeve stand watching the ball sail off into the distance.)

MAEVE: You threw it over the church tower!

UNA: See if you can catch that, little sister!

(Maeve dashes offstage left; Una kneels at down center and mimes sniffing flowers.)

UNA: These flowers are so beautiful. If they could speak, I wonder what they would say? Oh, daffodils, daffodils, pretty and fine, what secrets are locked in your petals sublime?

(SOUND: wind whistling offstage left mixed with Maeve's cries.)

MAEVE: *(o.s.)* No! No! Help, someone help me!

UNA: *(jumps up)* Maeve! Where are you? Where have you gone?

(Wind noise fades out. Una runs across stage left then right then back to center; QUEEN EMER enters from left and crosses to down center.)

UNA: Thank goodness, it is my mother, Queen Emer! She will know what to do! Mother!

QUEEN EMER: What is it, child?

UNA: Maeve has vanished!

QUEEN EMER: Vanished?

UNA: She has been gone over an hour!

QUEEN EMER: What happened?

UNA: We were playing toss-and-catch, and I threw the ball over the church tower. Maeve went to get the ball, and she — she has simply vanished!

QUEEN EMER: This is not another trick you two girls are playing, is it?

UNA: No, mother! I heard Maeve crying for help! I think something terrible has happened to her!

QUEEN EMER: Then we must find her right away. I will call the wisest person in the kingdom. Cormac! Come hither and give us counsel!

(SPOTLIGHT ON Cormac standing down right, facing audience.)

CORMAC: I am here, oh, queen. What have you to ask of me?

QUEEN EMER: My daughter Maeve has vanished after seeking her ball behind the church tower. Where has she gone?

UNA: Tell us where she has gone, noble druid, and I will bring her back!

CORMAC: Easier said than done. Alas, the poor girl must have gone round the church tower "widdershins."

UNA: Widdershins? What's that?

CORMAC: Widdershins is going in a circle from west to east, contrary to the way the sun travels. If this be true, your sister was carried off to Elfland by the Goblin King.

QUEEN EMER: Can she be saved?

CORMAC: The Goblin King is the most evil and cunning fairy in the universe. Not even the boldest knight in Erin would venture to Elfland.

UNA: Well, I am going to! It is my fault she ran round the church tower. Thus, I am going to save her!

QUEEN EMER: I see you are determined. Cormac, can you give Una any protection for this dangerous journey?

CORMAC: Behind the church tower, you will find a shillelagh. Take this and carry it with you at all times. And then you must remember two things. The first is that once you are in Elfland, no matter how hungry or thirsty you may become, you must eat no bite and drink no drop. The second is that everyone in Elfland, no matter how kind and pleasant they may appear, is a goblin and evil enchanter. If anyone speaks to you, you must kill them.

UNA: Kill them? But how?

CORMAC: By pointing your shillelagh at them and reciting these words — "Goblins grim and goblins hushed, I bid you shatter in flame and dust!"

(SPOTLIGHT OUT; Cormac exits right; Una kneels before Queen Emer, who places her hands on top of Una's head.)

UNA: A shillelagh? I am going to kill goblins with a simple shillelagh? Why, mother, that is no more than a crooked old stick! Cormac must be joking!

QUEEN EMER: A druid does not engage in folly. You must have faith in his words, or you and your sister will be lost.

UNA: But, mother!

QUEEN EMER: *(points right)* Go! Our kingdom prays for your safe return!

(Una exits right; LIGHTS OUT as Queen Emer exits left. LIGHTS UP FULL as HORSEHERD enters from left and crosses to down center. SOUND: horses neighing. Una enters from right, carrying the shillelagh.)

UNA: I have been wandering the forest for many hours, dragging this silly shillelagh! And as yet, not one sign of my sister or the Goblin king.

(Una sees Horseherd and pauses.)

UNA: Hark! It is a horseherd tending a pair of coal black

horses. And no ordinary horses, these! Look at their eyes! Filled with red sparks and blazing fire! Surely, I am in Elfland! *(approaches Horseherd)* Say there, Horseherd! Can you tell me where the King of Elfland resides?

HORSEHERD: *(cackles)* Hee-hee-hee-hee! I cannot tell thee, young maiden. But go on a wee bit farther and thou might find a cowherd who will. Hee-hee-hee-hee!

UNA: I do not like the mocking, mischievous smirk upon the lips of this Horseherd.

(Una circles around Horseherd until she is on his left; she points the shillelagh at his head.)

HORSEHERD: What is the matter, missy? Has thou not ever seen horses with the eyes of the devil? Hee-hee-hee-hee!

UNA: Goblins grim and goblins hushed, I bid you shatter in flame and dust!

HORSEHERD: *(screams)* Aiieeee!

(Horseherd falls to knees and crawls/rolls offstage left.)

UNA: He burst apart right before my eyes! Truly, the enchantments in Elfland are terrible and strong! And truly, this shillelagh is powerful, indeed!

(Una walks around the stage, as COWHERD enters from left. SOUND: cattle mooing.)

UNA: It is a cowherd driving cattle. And look at their horns! Why, they more resemble dancing skeletons than livestock! Surely, this is another goblin trick! *(approaches Cowherd)* Say there, Cowherd! Can you tell me where the King of Elfland resides?

COWHERD: *(cackles)* Hee-hee-hee-hee! I cannot tell thee,

young maiden. But go on a wee bit farther and thou might find a henwife who will. Hee-hee-hee-hee!

UNA: This Cowherd speaks with a most disrespectful tone.

(Una points the shillelagh at his head.)

COWHERD: What is the matter, missy? Has thou not ever seen cattle with the horns of the devil? Hee-hee-hee-hee!

UNA: Goblins grim and goblins hushed, I bid you shatter in flame and dust!

COWHERD: *(screams)* Aiieeee!

(Cowherd falls to knees and crawls/rolls offstage left.)

UNA: I have killed two goblins, yet I am no closer to finding my sister.

(Una walks around the stage, as HENWIFE, a shroud covering her face, enters from left. SOUND: chickens cackling. Una sees Henwife and pauses.)

UNA: It is a henwife feeding her chickens. Listen to them! Gibbering like web-footed demons! But this old woman appears so kind and harmless. I will see if she speaks. *(approaches Henwife)* Say there, Henwife! Can you tell me where the King of Elfland resides?

(Henwife says nothing but points left as Una circles her.)

UNA: She does not speak. This is an excellent omen. Henwife, I have heard the Goblin King lives in a dark tower on top of a black mountain that rises almost to the stars. Is this true?

(Henwife says nothing but nods "yes.")

UNA: And shall I find my sister a prisoner there?

(Henwife says nothing but nods "yes.")

UNA: I will go then to the Goblin King's tower. And when I arrive, I suppose I must walk round widdershins once, twice, three times.

(Henwife says nothing but nods "yes.")

UNA: Thank you, dear Henwife. I am off!

(Una stands behind Henwife.)

UNA: Oh, I must also say some magic words to open the tower door. I wonder what can they be?
HENWIFE: "Rood, nepo! Rood, nepo! Ni emoc em tel!"

(Una pulls down Henwife's shroud; Henwife snarls and crouches in a defensive posture, clawing the air, as Una points the shillelagh at her head.)

UNA: Ah-ha! I see by your flaming eyes that you *are* a goblin! You have spoken your last words of deceit! Goblins grim and goblins hushed, I bid you shatter in flame and dust!
HENWIFE: *(screams)* Aiieeee!

(Henwife falls to knees and crawls/rolls offstage left. Una spies the scrim at mid left.)

UNA: There is the dark tower of the Goblin King! *(crosses to scrim)* The goblin, disguised as a henwife, wanted me to walk widdershins round the tower. Then I shall walk the opposite. And what were the magic words to open the tower door? "Rood, nepo! Rood, nepo! Ni emoc em tel!"

Hmmm. Say them backwards, and they become "Open, door! Open door! Let me come in!" *(paces in front of the scrim three times)* Open, door! Open, door! Let me come in! Open, door! Open, door! Let me come in! *(stops in front of scrim)* By all the saints in heaven, the tower door is opening! I shall go inside!

(LIGHTS OUT BRIEFLY as Una goes behind the scrim on the left and reappears on the right; Maeve enters at up right and sits on stool. LIGHTS UP FULL. SOUND: wind whistling offstage left for a few seconds, then fades out.)

UNA: That sound! That dreadful sound of a goblin's raging breath! My, what a curious place this is! I see no windows and no candles, yet there is all about a shimmering light as if it were day. *(examines the scrim)* Why, the floor and ceiling are made of crystal rock! And all the walls are encrusted with silver, gold, and sparkling gems of all kinds! *(walks around to down left)* How can an evil creature like the Goblin King live in such beauty and splendor?

MAEVE: *(singsong)* I can throw farther than Una! I can throw farther than Una!

UNA: *(turns toward Maeve's voice)* The voice of my sister! She is here! Maeve! Where are you? Maeve!

(Una crosses to center stage, sees Maeve and approaches her cautiously.)

UNA: Maeve? Is that you sitting on a couch of velvet and gold?

MAEVE: It is me, Una! How wonderful that you are here! Come sit in this delightful room filled with pearls and rubies! *(singsong)* I can throw farther than Una! I can throw farther than Una!

UNA: This is indeed a beautiful room. But, my sister, I fear you are under the Goblin King's spell.

MAEVE: Nonsense! You are tired and hungry. Would you like something to eat?

UNA: Yes, I am quite hungry. But how will you find food in this place?

MAEVE: You simply have to wish for it, and it appears.

(Maeve pulls out a bowl from under the stool.)

MAEVE: You wished for a bowl of delicious mutton stew. Here it is!

(Una takes bowl, raises it to her lips and is about to sip from it.)

UNA: What was the first thing Cormac said I must remember? "Once in Elfland, no matter how hungry or thirsty you may become, you must eat no bite and drink no drop." *(flings bowl offstage right)* Away from me, cursed stew!

(LIGHTS FLASH. SOUND: wind whistling offstage left for a few seconds, then fades out. THE GOBLIN KING enters from left, followed by FOUR GOBLINS; they have swords at their sides. Una turns and sees them.)

UNA: It is the Goblin King and his minions! Vile creature, let my sister go!

GOBLIN KING: Our new guest does not wish to eat! Very well, then — she shall be eaten! *(cackles)* Hee-hee-hee-hee!

FOUR GOBLINS: Kill her! Kill her! Eat her! Eat her!

(Una advances boldly and points the shillelagh at them.)

UNA: Goblins grim and goblins hushed, I bid you shatter in

flame and dust! (*pause, Goblins remain standing*) Goblins grim and goblins hushed, I bid you shatter in flame and dust! (*pause, Goblins remain standing*) Nothing happens! The goblins still stand!

(*Four Goblins and Goblin King laugh and shriek.*)

GOBLIN KING: Your pathetic spells are useless in my tower domain. Draw your swords, goblins, our supper is at hand!

(*Four Goblins draw their swords and encircle Una at mid center, dancing and cavorting as the Goblin King watches and laughs.*)

UNA: I call upon all saints and druids! Give me the power to defeat this hideous host!

(*LIGHTS FLASH FOR SEVERAL SECONDS.*)

UNA: My shillelagh has turned into a golden sword! Goblins fierce and goblins foul, this blade is going to make you howl!

(*Una attacks the Four Goblins with her shillelagh/ sword; she defeats them one by one, and they fall to the ground. She faces the Goblin King at down center.*)

UNA: Now it is your turn, Goblin King!

GOBLIN KING: (*draws his sword*) Observe my sword changing into a towering serpent, hissing and coiling, as it readies a poisonous blow. There is no magic you possess that can defeat the Goblin King of Elfland!

UNA: Oh, but there is! Power of raven, power of crake, make my sword cut through this snake!

(Una slashes at the Goblin King's sword and knocks it out of his hand.)

GOBLIN KING: My sword!

(Una shoves her shillelegh against the Goblin King's chest.)

UNA: Goblin cruel and goblin frayed, end your life upon this blade!

(Goblin King pulls Una's shillelagh into him, killing himself.)

GOBLIN KING: *(screams, falls to ground)* Aiieeee!

(Maeve jumps up.)

MAEVE: Una! Help!

(Maeve and Una meet at mid center.)

MAEVE: Where am I? What terrible place is this?
UNA: It is the tower of the Goblin King. And see how all the gems are turning black!
MAEVE: All the beauty was but illusion!
UNA: Now that the Goblin King is dead, his dark realm of lies is collapsing! Quick, we must flee!

(Maeve and Una exit left; SPOTLIGHT ON CORMAC standing down right, facing audience.)

CORMAC: And that is the story of how brave Una rescued her sister Maeve from the Goblin King. After many more adventures, the two maidens finally arrived home, where their mother the Queen welcomed them with a wonderful feast.

(LIGHTS UP FULL on Queen Emer, Maeve and Una walking onstage from left and standing at down center, facing audience)

QUEEN EMER: And I hope you two girls have learned a valuable lesson.

MAEVE: I will never run round a church widdershins again!

UNA: *(raises shillelagh)* And I will never doubt the power of the humblest tool to accomplish the biggest task.

(LIGHTS OUT.)

THE END

Young Olli and the Trolls

This humorous tale from Finland incorporates the popular "youngest sibling" motif, where the youngest son or daughter is considered to be a simpleton but ends up outwitting everyone and usually saving his older brothers or sisters. The cannibalistic ogre who falls into its own trap is also found in fairy tales around the globe, from Hungary and Portugal to India, Persia and Southern Africa. The ogre in this tale, the dwarfish *troll,* is a supernatural being common to Scandinavian folklore and appears under various names throughout the world of faerydom — *brownies* (Scotland), *domavoi* (Russia), *pixies* (Cornwall), *jin* (Middle East), *fata* (Italy), *batua* (Central Africa), *leprechauns* (Ireland), *nats* (Burma). Trolls typically guard stolen treasure, terrorize humans and burst if the sun shines on them.

RUNNING TIME: 20 minutes

PLACE: Finland

CAST: 13 actors, min. 5 boys, 5 girls

Olli	Illi, Olli's Elder Brother
Olli's Father	Ulli, Olli's Eldest Brother
Olli's Mother	Old Troll
Mrs. Troll	3 Troll Daughters
Troll's Horse	2 Troll Neighbors

STAGE SET: 2 stools at down right; kitchen table and 2 chairs at mid center — the table has a cloth that comes down in front to floor to conceal area under table; a large, oven-shaped cardboard box with flaps at mid left

PROPS: newspaper, knitting needles, knitting, purse of coins, several small bags of coins, pot, spoon, 3 blue stocking caps, 3 white stocking caps, long knife, horse bridle, drill, bucket, pillow, serving plate, necklace bead

COSTUMES: Humans and Trolls wear simple medieval peasant clothes; Trolls have hideous face masks and Mrs. Troll wears a bead necklace; Troll's Horse should have a gold and silver covering for torso and mane

PERFORMANCE NOTE: when goblins, witches, trolls, etc. "burst apart" or die from rays of the sun or magic swords and so forth, they can fling confetti in the air to symbolize their dissolution into smithereens

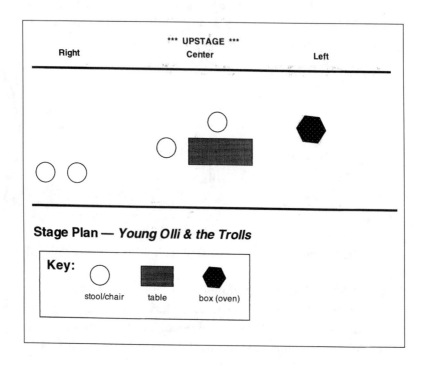

Stage Plan — *Young Olli & the Trolls*

Key: ◯ stool/chair   ▬ table   ⬡ box (oven)

(LIGHTS UP RIGHT on OLLI'S FATHER and OLLI'S MOTHER sitting on stools at down right; Olli's Father reads a newspaper, Olli's Mother knits.)

OLLI'S FATHER: *(to audience)* Why, hello there! *(to Olli's Mother)* Look, Greta, these must be the new neighbors!

OLLI'S MOTHER: Of course, they're the new neighbors, Pekka. They just moved in yesterday from Helsinki.

OLLI'S FATHER: Helsinki! Hey-hey! Brights lights, big city! *(chuckles)* Well, you'll find it pretty quiet out here in the country. Pardon? Did we know *who*? People, what people? Oh, *those* people, the people who lived in your house before you did. Wellllll, they were, uh... *(to Olli's Mother)* You think we should tell them about, the, you know, the—

OLLI'S MOTHER: Honestly, Pekka, I'm not a mind reader! Speak up for goodness sake! *(to audience)* You'll have to excuse him, he's been off his curds and whey lately.

OLLI'S FATHER: Well, to put it simply, the people who lived next door were what you'd call — Trolls.

(LIGHTS UP CENTER and LEFT on an OLD TROLL and his wife, MRS. TROLL, seated at the kitchen table at mid center. The Old Troll is gleefully counting coins in a money purse; Mrs. Troll is stirring something in a pot with a spoon.)

OLD TROLL: *(sniffs air)* My, that is an appetizing aroma! What's for dinner, Mrs. Troll?

MRS. TROLL: Your favorite, dear. Mashed baby brains and brazed leg of farmer.

OLD TROLL: Mmmmmm...delicious!

OLLI'S FATHER: Those Trolls were really nasty. They ate people for breakfast, lunch, dinner and in-between meal snacks.

(OLLI, ILLI and ULLI enter from right and stand to the left of Olli's Father and Olli's Mother.)

OLLI'S FATHER: Ah, here come my young sons! This is Ulli, my eldest.

(Ulli bows to audience.)

OLLI'S FATHER: Illi, my second eldest.

(Illi bows to audience.)

OLLI'S FATHER: And Olli, the youngest. The one who most resembles his mother.
OLLI'S MOTHER: He's also the cleverest.

(Olli bows to audience.)

OLLI'S FATHER: I say, lads. Now that you've reached man- hood, it's time for you to do something about the Trolls who live on the mountain next door.
ULLI: What about them?
OLLI'S FATHER: What about them? Well, they're cannibals, for one thing! And for another they're incredibly rich, even though they're wicked. They've got piles of gold and jewels hidden away, which they've stolen from the rest of the neighbors over the years.
ILLI: I always thought they were kinda creepy. What do you want us to do?
OLLI'S FATHER: Do? Am I going to have to write a book and print it on your forehead?
OLLI'S MOTHER: Your father would like you to go to the Trolls, steal their riches and then kill them, if it's not too much trouble.
OLLI: You bet! Let's go, guys!
ULLI: Hey, hey, hey, youngster! You're the baby of the family.

Illi and I will be the ones who rout out that old Troll, and you can watch us do it!

(OLLI, ILLI and ULLI walk around the stage and come to the table at center, standing a few feet to the right.)

OLLI'S FATHER: So the three brothers journeyed over the mountain and just after sunset, they came to the house of the Trolls.

ILLI: Here we are! I'll just knock—

ULLI: No you won't. I'm the eldest. I'll knock.

ILLI: You're the doofiest! I took door-knocking in school!

ULLI: You wouldn't know which end of the door to knock!

OLLI: *(knocks on door)* Knock, knock, knock!

MRS. TROLL: Somebody is at the door, dear. Can you please see who it is?

OLD TROLL: *(rises slowly)* If it's another thatch siding salesman, I'm going to be verrrrry angry!

MRS. TROLL: Just invite him in, dear, and we'll have him for supper! *(giggles)*

OLD TROLL: *(opens door)* Yes?

ILLI: Hello! We are your neighbors from over the mountain. My name is Illi.

ULLI: My name is Ulli.

OLLI: And my name is—

ILLI: Just our kid brother, Olli.

OLD TROLL: Neighbors, eh? I suppose you've come about my daughters.

ULLI: Huh? What daughters?

ILLI: Trolls have daughters?

OLD TROLL: Of course, Trolls have daughters. As a matter of fact, I have three beautiful daughters who desperately need husbands. And, of course, whoever marries them will inherit all my riches.

ULLI: *(to Illi)* Did he say what I think he said?

ILLI: *(to Ulli)* It sounds like a great deal. We won't have to kill the Trolls to get their riches. We can just marry their daughters.

OLLI: Uhhh, brothers, hold on a second. I don't think we should just jump right into this.

ULLI: *(to Old Troll)* Did you say, we'd inherit *all* your riches?

OLD TROLL: Every last gold coin!

ILLI: Whoo-hoo! Bring on those big, beautiful Troll daughters!

(THREE TROLL DAUGHTERS enter from left and curtsey; Ulli, Illi and Olli bow in return.)

TROLL DAUGHTER #1: I'm Trulla. My favorite color is red, as in dripping blood.

TROLL DAUGHTER #2: I'm Trilla. I like to eat small animals feet-first.

TROLL DAUGHTER #3: I'm Trolla. I sometimes lay in a dark cave for days.

MRS. TROLL: Come, come, enough small talk; let's all sit down to supper. We've got three wonderful weddings to plan!

(Daughters and Brothers gather around table and mime eating.)

OLLI'S FATHER: Actually, they were planning three funerals. The Trolls were going to kill the brothers and eat them. So, after a hearty supper, the Trolls sent the daughters and the brothers into the parlor to get ready for bed.

(Daughters and Brothers stretch out on floor at down left; they lay on their backs, alternating Daughter and Brother, Olli on the extreme left.)

MRS. TROLL: Now, you young folks just settle down and go to sleep. *(to Old Troll)* Dear, hand our guests their sleeping caps.

(Old Troll hands a blue stocking cap to each of the Brothers; the Daughters put on their own white stocking caps.)

ULLI: Gosh, souvenirs!

ILLI: These are really neat, Mrs. Troll!

MRS. TROLL: You boys look so handsome in those blue caps. And see, our daughters have matching white caps.

ULLI: Cool!

OLLI: *(to Troll Daughter #3)* Would you like to trade caps?

OLD TROLL: No, no! No cap-trading! You boys have to wear your own caps before the wedding. Then you can trade.

ILLI: *(pokes Olli)* Yeh, squirt, keep your own cap. Are you trying to get us in trouble with these Troll girls?

MRS. TROLL: Nighty-night! Sleep tight! Don't let the bedbugs bite! *(giggles)*

(Old Troll and Mrs. Troll sit at table and put heads on table; Brothers and Daughters lay down on floor, Ulli and Illi snoring loudly. LIGHTS CENTER AND LEFT FADE DOWN TO LOW; Olli sits up, looks around, then rises and quickly exchanges the blue caps with the white ones before lying down again.)

OLLI'S MOTHER: When everyone was asleep, Olli got up and changed the caps. He took the blue caps he and his brothers were wearing and put them on the Troll daughters.

OLLI'S FATHER: Then he took the daughters' white caps and put them on his brothers and himself.

OLLI'S MOTHER: Smart boy, my young Olli.

(Old Troll awakes, stretches, picks up a long knife and

crosses to above where the Daughters and Brothers are sleeping.)

OLD TROLL: Blue caps, blue caps, rum-a-tum-tum! You'll be supper tonight, yum-yum! My goodness, it's dark in here! Ah, there's a blue cap. *(whacks knife on floor)*

TROLL DAUGHTER #1: Oww!

OLD TROLL: There's one! *(whacks knife on floor)*

TROLL DAUGHTER #2: Oww!

OLD TROLL: There's two! *(whacks knife on floor)*

TROLL DAUGHTER #3: Oww!

OLD TROLL: And there's number three!

(Old Troll picks up blue caps and returns to table, where he goes back to sleep; Olli rises, wakes Ulli and Illi; the three Brothers tiptoe across the stage to down right. LIGHTS FADE OUT CENTER AND LEFT as Three Troll Daughters exit left.)

OLLI'S MOTHER: When Olli heard the Old Troll sleeping again, he roused Ulli and Illi and told them what had happened. They snuck out of the Troll house and were back home by morning.

OLLI'S FATHER: Boy oh boy, I bet old man Troll was mad when he found out he'd chopped off the heads of his daughters! So, when are you lads going back for the riches?

ULLI: Going back? You must be mad!

ILLI: Pop, those Trolls almost killed us!

OLLI'S MOTHER: And certainly would have, if it hadn't been for the cleverness of your young brother.

OLLI: I've heard the Troll has a horse with a mane of gold and silver. Let's bring it back here!

ULLI: And get my head cut off? No way!

ILLI: If you were as mature as Ulli and I, you wouldn't even think of doing something so foolish.

OLLI: All right, you stay home. But the next time you see me, I'll be riding the Troll's horse.
ULLI & ILLI: Yeh, yeh, sure, sure...

(Ulli and Illi exit right as LIGHTS FADE OUT RIGHT. Olli walks around stage and comes to the table at center, standing a few feet to the right. LIGHTS UP CENTER AND LEFT.)

OLLI: *(knocks on door)* Knock, knock, knock!

(Mrs. Troll enters from left and pauses at down left, spying Olli at the door.)

MRS. TROLL: Dear me, it's that terrible Finnish boy, the one that changed the caps! And wouldn't you know, my husband is out terrorizing the village!
OLLI: *(knocks on door)* Knock, knock, knock!
MRS. TROLL: Come in! *(to audience)* I'll just have to keep him occupied till the Old Troll comes home and can devour him.

(Olli walks up to the table, as Mrs. Troll motions him to sit.)

MRS. TROLL: Why, it's Olli, isn't it? Sit down, sit down. Just passing through the neighborhood, were you?
OLLI: *(sits)* Yes, Mrs. Troll. I was wondering how your daughters were doing today.
MRS. TROLL: They're not doing so well.
OLLI: I'm sorry to hear that. I hope my brothers and I didn't say anything to offend them.
MRS. TROLL: No, they just came down with very bad headaches.
OLLI: There's a lot of that going around. I suppose they'll be up and around soon enough.

MRS. TROLL: Actually, they're dead. But thank you for asking.

OLLI: Oh. Well, I guess I'd better be on my way. *(stands)*

MRS. TROLL: Oh, oh, oh! Can't you stay a little bit longer? I have some delicious gristle-bone pie!

OLLI: No thanks. I have chores to do.

MRS. TROLL: Well, could you do a chore for me before you go? Take my husband's horse down to the lake and give him a good watering.

OLLI: Gee, Mrs. Troll, that would be swell.

MRS. TROLL: Thank you so much. *(whistles for Horse)* Here, horsie, here, boy!

(TROLL'S HORSE enters from left and whinnies.)

TROLL'S HORSE: Neighhhhhhhhh!

MRS. TROLL: This is our neigbor Olli. He's going to take you for a walk and water you.

TROLL'S HORSE: Neighhhhhhhhh!

(Troll's Horse trots over to Olli, who takes him by the bridle and leads him to down right.)

OLLI: I won't be very long.

MRS. TROLL: Take all the time you want, Olli! *(to audience)* By the time my husband comes home, Olli will be tired and ready to sleep and then — *(makes a cutting motion across her throat)* Olli-burgers for a week! *(exits left, cackling)* Hee-hee-hee-hee-hee…

(LIGHTS OUT CENTER AND LEFT; LIGHTS UP RIGHT on Olli's Father and Olli's Mother seated down right, as Olli stands with the Troll's Horse.)

OLLI'S FATHER: Let me get this straight. You have stolen the Troll's Horse?

OLLI: Not exactly, Pop. Mrs. Troll asked me to take the horse down to the lake and give him a good watering. So I did. And in payment for my labor, I'm going to keep the horse.

TROLL'S HORSE: Neighhhhhhhhh!

OLLI'S MOTHER: It's a fair exchange. The nerve of that woman, asking our Olli to do Troll chores!

TROLL'S HORSE: Neighhhhhhhhh!

OLLI'S FATHER: But the Old Troll is going to be very angry when he finds out Olli has stolen — sorry, "taken" — his horse with the gold and silver mane, and that after killing his daughters.

TROLL'S HORSE: Neighhhhhhhhh!

OLLI'S FATHER: Can this horse say anything besides, "Neighhhhhhhhh!"?

TROLL'S HORSE: Of course, I can. I'm a magic horse, after all. You want I should recite the Finnish yellow pages?

OLLI: Give this horse to my brothers. I'm going back and get the Troll's money purse and all his ill-gotten riches.

OLLI'S MOTHER: That's my Olli!

OLLI'S FATHER: I'm sure his riches are well hidden! How will you find them?

OLLI: I won't have to. The Troll will show them to me.

TROLL'S HORSE: Neighhhhhhhhh!

OLLI'S FATHER: I couldn't have said it better myself!

(LIGHTS OUT RIGHT; LIGHTS UP LEFT AND CENTER; Old Troll and Mrs. Troll are asleep at the kitchen table. Olli creeps behind them, carrying a drill and a bucket and kneels a couple feet behind and to their left.)

OLLI: *(to audience)* Here is a lesson from my new book: "How to Drive Trolls Crazy in Seven Steps." Step one, late at night crawl up on the roof of their house. Step two, drill a hole above their bedroom. *(points drill at the floor and begins drilling motions)* Step three, pour water through the hole. *(mimes pouring water from the bucket)* Step four, make like a hurricane from the North Pole! Whooooooo! Whooooooo! Whooooooo!

(Old Troll and Mrs. Troll splutter awake.)

MRS. TROLL: A terrible storm has arisen! Our bed is soaked!

OLD TROLL: It must be a hurricane! *(jumps up)*

MRS. TROLL: Hurricane? There are no hurricanes in Finland! *(ducks under the table)*

OLD TROLL: There's always a first time for everything!

MRS. TROLL: What are you doing underneath the table?

OLD TROLL: I'm saving our riches from the hurricane! Quick, help me before they're swept away!

(Old Troll pulls up several bags of coins and puts them on the table; Olli stands up and waves at Mrs. Troll, catching her attention.)

MRS. TROLL: Oh no! It's that pesky Finnish boy again!

OLD TROLL: What! Catch him before he flees!

(Mrs. Troll and Old Troll grab Olli, who makes no resistance but simply smiles.)

OLLI: I was just passing by and saw the light —

OLD TROLL: Thief! You stole my gold-and-silver horse!

MRS. TROLL: And gave our daughters very bad headaches!

OLLI: Guilty as charged. I suppose you'd better punish me.

OLD TROLL: Punish you? Ha! We'll cook you!

MRS. TROLL: And eat you!

OLLI: I certainly hope so. In fact, why don't we make a party out of the occasion?

OLD TROLL: A party?

MRS. TROLL: He's right, husband. We could invite the

neighbor Trolls from across the lake. It's been ages since we've seen them.

OLLI: You could have a barbecue!

OLD TROLL: What an excellent idea!

OLLI: I quite agree!

OLD TROLL: *(grips Olli's shoulder)* He is very young and tender. Quick, wife, you fire up the oven, and I'll summon the neighbors for a feast — of roast Finn! *(laughs)* Ha-ha-ha!

(Old Troll exits left; Mrs. Troll busily mimes putting wood into fire in front of oven/box at mid left as Olli slips the coin bags into his jacket.)

MRS. TROLL: Now, Olli, you sit down while the fire heats. I'll just cut up a few vegetables.

OLLI: Can I be of any help?

MRS. TROLL: Oh, no, no, no. You relax and save your strength. We want you as fresh as possible. *(hums)* Da-dee-da-da-dee-dum…*(singsong)* Oh, we're going to eat young Olli, from his head to his tippy-tippy toes!

OLLI: Is the oven ready?

MRS. TROLL: Why, yes, it looks as if it is! Come over and get in like a good lad.

(Olli gets up and squats in front of the box; he struggles to get in but cannot.)

MRS. TROLL: Not that way! Straighten up! No, hunch over! There you go! No, not that way! To the left, to the left! No! Oh, you are such an awkward boy!

OLLI: I'm sorry. Perhaps you can show me the correct way to get into the oven.

MRS. TROLL: Very well. Stand aside.

(Mrs. Troll pushes him aside and hunches herself in front of the box with her head facing the opening.)

MRS. TROLL: Olli, it's really very simple. Watch closely, so you'll know how to do it when it's your turn. Tuck your head in like so…then, scrunch your arms up alongside…
OLLI: And then you're ready to go in?
MRS. TROLL: Ready to go and shut the door!

(Olli pushes her into the box and shuts the flaps.)

MRS. TROLL: *(screams)* Aiiieeeee!
OLLI: You were right, Mrs. Troll. It really is very simple. See you at supper!

(Olli reaches under the table and draws out a serving plate he places on the table; he then draws out a large pillow, with the top of the pillow having eyes, nose and mouth drawn on it to resemble a person.)

OLLI: Step five, set the table for your guests. Step six, make sure your hostess is well seasoned.

(Olli sets the pillow up behind the oven, then exits right as Old Troll and TWO TROLL NEIGHBORS enter from left and cross to table.)

OLD TROLL: *(sniffs air)* My, that is an appetizing aroma! Come in, neighbors, and let's eat our young Finn!

(Two Troll Neighbors sit at table, while Old Troll peers around.)

TROLL NEIGHBOR #1: Look, the food is already on the table!
TROLL NEIGHBOR #2: What a thoughtful wife you have, Old Troll! Where is she?

OLD TROLL: There she is behind the oven.

TROLL NEIGHBOR #1: She must be resting. Cooking a hardy young human is a taxing chore.

TROLL NEIGHBOR #2: I'm starved. Can we begin?

OLD TROLL: By all means, dig in, dig in! But don't forget to save some for the Missus!

(Troll Neighbors and Old Troll mime eating with hands as if gnawing on drumsticks.)

TROLL NEIGHBOR #1: Mmmm-mmmm-delicious! Mrs. Troll has provided a truly special repast!

TROLL NEIGHBOR #2: Indeed, this is the best roast Finn I've had in months! Awwwk! *(bites down on something hard and holds his mouth)*

TROLL NEIGHBOR #1: What's wrong with you?

TROLL NEIGHBOR #2: *(pulls a bead from his mouth)* I nearly choked on this...this bead.

OLD TROLL: Let me see that. *(examines bead)* Why, that bead is from my wife's favorite necklace!

(Troll Neighbor #1 pokes around on plate, stops and grimaces.)

TROLL NEIGHBOR #1: Would this be a cornea from your wife's favorite eyeball?

OLD TROLL: Let me see that! *(examines plate)* Curses! We haven't been eating that rascal Olli! We've been eating my wife! Do you know what this means?

TROLL NEIGHBOR #2: The party is over?

OLD TROLL: It means besides killing my wife, he's also stolen my riches, which were right here on this table! We must find him at once!

(Troll Neighbors do not move.)

TROLL NEIGHBOR #1: You know, this sort of dish doesn't go well as leftovers.

OLD TROLL: Very well, finish your meal, you gluttons! I'm going to find that terrible Olli!

(Old Troll dashes offstage left as Olli creeps onstage from right; Troll Neighbors carry off plate and exit left as Olli pauses at up center.)

OLLI: Old Troll! Old Troll! I've been looking for you all night! Where are you Old Troll?

(Old Troll creeps onstage from left, peering around wildly.)

OLD TROLL: I know you're out there, Olli! Ah-ha!

(Old Troll spies Olli and approaches him, knife in hand; Olli also approaches and they chase around the kitchen table before stopping on opposite sides, Olli facing left, Old Troll facing right.)

OLD TROLL: You killed my daughters!

OLLI: Begging your pardon, Old Troll, but technically it was *you* who cut their heads off.

OLD TROLL: You stole my horse!

OLLI: He was given to me.

OLD TROLL: You stole all my riches!

OLLI: The riches you stole from honest Finns!

OLD TROLL: And you killed and cooked my wife!

OLLI: *(points behind Old Troll)* Wait! Is that her over there?

(Old Troll turns; SPOTLIGHT ON Old Troll, who screams and falls as he is caught in the rays of the rising sun.)

OLD TROLL: Aiiieeeee! *(quivers and dies)*

OLLI: I guess not. It's the morning sun. And that's step seven — keep the Troll chasing you all night, so that when he finally catches you, it's dawn, and he's vaporized into a smudge puddle!

(SPOTLIGHT OUT; LIGHTS FADE UP RIGHT as Olli crosses to down right, bowing to his parents before exiting right.)

OLLI'S FATHER: So long, son. Keep up the good work.

OLLI'S MOTHER: *(to audience)* So, I think you'll like the neighborhood. It's a lot quieter now that the Trolls are gone.

OLLI'S FATHER: Much quieter. No screaming. No howling.

OLLI'S MOTHER: You got a great bargain on the house. The Trolls may have been cannibals, but they kept the property in very good shape.

OLLI'S FATHER: Very good shape. Just make sure...well, ummm, hmmm, uhhh...

OLLI'S MOTHER: Honestly, Pekka, we're not mind readers! Speak up for goodness sake! Just make sure *what?*

OLLI'S FATHER: Well, before you do any cooking — just make sure to clean out the oven.

(LIGHTS OUT.)

THE END

THE AUTHOR

L.E. McCULLOUGH, PH.D. is a playwright, composer and ethnomusicologist whose studies in music and folklore have spanned cultures throughout the world. Formerly Assistant Director of the Indiana University School of Music at Indianapolis and a touring artist with Young Audiences, Inc., Dr. McCullough is the Administrative Director of the Humanities Theatre Group at Indiana University-Purdue University at Indianapolis. Winner of the 1995 Playwrights' Preview Productions Emerging Playwright Award for his stage play *Blues for Miss Buttercup,* he is the author of *The Complete Irish Tinwhistle Tutor, Favorite Irish Session Tunes* and *St. Patrick Was a Cajun,* three highly acclaimed music instruction books, and has performed on the soundtracks for the PBS specials *The West* and *Lewis and Clark.* Since 1991 Dr. McCullough has received 35 awards in 26 national literary competitions and had 178 poem and short story publications in 90 North American literary journals. He is a member of The Dramatists Guild, Inc. and the American Conference for Irish Studies.